EXPECTING REFERRALS

To Errol + James,

I wish you both all the best of life

Scott Kramnick

EXPECTING REFERRALS:

THE RESURRECTION OF A LOST ART

by

SCOTT KRAMNICK

ASSOCIATES PUBLISHING   ●   VIRGINIA

Associates Publishing
4300 Plank Road, Suite 280
Fredericksburg, Virginia 22407
703-786-9799

Third Edition

Printed and bound in the United States of
America.

Graphics by Select Marketing
Printed by The William Byrd Press,
Richmond, Virginia

Library of Congress Cataloging-in-Publication
Data

Kramnick, Scott A.
Expecting referrals: the resurrection of a lost
art / Scott A. Kramnick. -- 3rd ed.
p. cm.
Includes Index.
1. Selling. 2. Business -- Communication
systems. 3. Social networks. I. Title.
HF5438.25.K718   1994   94-10547
658.85--dc20
                                        CIP
ISBN 0-9638953-1-1

To

Elizabeth,

Elena,

and

Ziggy...

I miss you.

ACKNOWLEDGMENTS

The most difficult task of recognizing the many people who have helped shape my ideas and contributed to my ability to write this book begins here. The first person who comes to mind (as she had better) is my lovely wife, Tricia. She has never wavered in her support and has been the pillar of strength I have always counted on. I thank my son Jason, for keeping me company and making me smile when I might otherwise frown. To my son Jonathan, whose first word will not be "mama" or "dada" but will be "referral," I love you. To Ray Porter, Lt. Col. USMC (Ret.), who rescued me from the "benjo" ditches of Okinawa and introduced me to life, thank you. To Harry "Skip" Larsen, whose common sense suggestions have made this book comprehensible, thank you for being so tactful! To the late Napoleon Hill whose book, *Think and Grow Rich*, taught me that thoughts **are** things .... They Are. To Bill Buttram who encouraged me to buy *Think and Grow Rich*, your advice was picture perfect. I thank Allen Kidd, Becky Biddle, Roger Arnold and Mike Masterson for their guidance and support when my business was in its infancy. To Daniel Porter who has grown with me from the beginning and has always been here: I value our friendship, thank you. To my good friend in Fredericksburg who is as unselfish with himself as he is with his knowledge, thank you for believing in me. "You're really, really not a bad guy!" To my clients who have trusted me with their well-being ... I will never let you down.

"It is not the critic who counts, not the man who points out how the strong man stumbled or where the doer of deeds could have done better. The credit belongs to the man who is actually in the arena; whose face is marred by dust and sweat and blood; who strives valiantly; who errs and comes short again and again ... who knows the great enthusiasms, the great devotions, and spends himself in a worthy cause; who at the least knows in the end the triumph of high achievement; and who, at the worst, if he fails, at least fails while doing greatly, so that his place shall never be with those cold and timid souls who know neither victory nor defeat."

- *Theodore Roosevelt*

Table of Contents

Foreword

At age twenty-nine, when disc surgery at two levels ended an eleven-year Marine Corps career, I found myself out on the street with a degree in Russian, a few medals, and a pretty good knowledge of various combat formations. Not wanting to sit behind a desk translating Russian newsletters, I had few skills to do much else.

I was told that sales was a lonely business. But with a wife and two children, I had to do something quickly. I began selling mutual funds and life insurance. I had lived in Virginia for only six months prior to my discharge from the Marine Corps. There were no friends or family to whom I could sell. After I made my first fifty cold calls, I realized that I would not be able to accept the rejection to which others in my profession had grown accustomed. I then began developing a method by which the few people that would see me would agree to give me referrals.

This book is the result of a four-year process that has evolved into a science. I have worked to perfec every detail of my referral generation process. For me, sales is not a lonely business. In fact, it is quite the opposite. Not only do I share the companionship of my associates with whom I work, but I also enjoy the friendships which have developed between my clients and me. Because of my referral system, I have grown very close to many of my clients who have been generous in referring many of their friends to me. It is easy to make friends with people who support you in business.

In an age of computer generated leads, junk mail and cold calls, most of the public dread the unsolicited telephone calls that interfere with their evenings of relaxation. Numerous individuals and organizations have testified before Congress seeking to outlaw some or all of these practices. The solution to this problem lies not in legislation but in both sensitizing salespeople toward the attitudes and emotions of the public and in teaching them the lost art of generating new leads through referrals. Over fourteen million salespeople in fields ranging from insurance, real estate and automobile sales, to Avon, Amway and Tupperware, are constantly prospecting for new clients. It is easy to understand the negative prejudices felt by most consumers.

The methodology contained in this book will allow salespeople to prospect more efficiently and with a higher level of self-esteem, while providing their customers with added value, greater service and improved relationships. Millions of customers anxiously await the end of the aggravation of unwanted intrusion by eager salespeople. Millions of salespeople are hungry for a better way of prospecting that allows them to be successful while eliminating the rejection to which they have grown so accustomed. This referral generation system gets you to the point where you can devote yourself to what you do best - sell.

The information contained in this book is not revolutionary in thought or design. It is, however, a method I have created which provides the detailed procedures required to bring us back to the days of old. It is my belief that in the near future success in sales will become totally dependent upon a salesperson's ability to get referrals. A half century ago this was a common practice which was perfected by many.

Unfortunately, like the lost city of Atlantis, the practice has been buried and forgotten by most. My purpose in writing this book is to part the waters and alter the rushing waves of overeager salespeople who have never been taught or have forgotten the most rewarding characteristic of our business.

The greatest reward is knowing that you are appreciated by your clients. Clients can show their appreciation in no greater way than by encouraging their friends, family and acquaintances to do business with you.

Every day, during the selling of products or services, billions of dollars change hands. Hundreds of thousands of sales transactions take place. As a salesperson you have a tremendous opportunity to have a positive impact upon the emotions of others. It is time for us resurrect the true care that we once had for our clients. If we do this, we will also resurrect the lost art of expecting referrals.

I owe my professional success to the hundreds of clients who have unselfishly given of themselves in helping play matchmaker between their acquaintances and me. I would like to thank them for keeping the faith while I once again pledge to continue to earn their trust.

Scott A. Kramnick
September, 1993

Introduction

I f you earn a living, the odds are high that your income is dependent in some form or another on the successful sale of a product or service. Although the design, value or benefit of a specific product is a critical factor in the consumer's decision making process, equally critical is the person and/or company selling the product. The purchaser's contact with the salesperson before the exchange of goods or services are completed gives the salesperson the opportunity to promote the value and benefits of the product in which the consumer has expressed interest.

Salespeople can use various methods to disseminate information about their products or services to prospective buyers. Door-to-door visitations, newspaper, yellow page, radio or television advertisements, letters and mailers, seminars, or the much dreaded "cold-calls" are among the most common and popular.

In my many discussions with salespeople across the country, I have learned that the major difficulty for everyone lies in getting enough opportunities to make presentations to prospective buyers. I have never been questioned about either the best method for presenting a product or service or which products or services to sell.

The question every salesperson asks me is "How do you get your prospects?" My answer is simple. Referrals.

I have been in the financial services industry for less than five years. Prior to that I was in the Marine Corps. My reason for telling you this is to let you know that I have had no previous sales experience. Often people who have been in sales for ten, fifteen or twenty years work primarily through referrals. Naturally, if a salesperson has stood the test of time and has built up a significant client base, information about the salesperson and the products or services offered will be known and respected within the community. The major problem is getting to see enough people in the early years so that you can be successful enough to remain in business for twenty years into the future, after which the job of prospecting becomes easier.

The purpose of this book is to teach a specific methodology for getting referrals. Most people in sales can gain by applying these principles to their own situation. The methods presented here will not require that you change your current sales technique. However, the specific procedures outlined in the coming chapters will enhance your ability to become more effective with your prospects and clients.

Throughout this book you will find dozens of scripts to help you apply the many specific recommendations with your prospects or clients. These scripts are set apart by a dark vertical bar and should be used as a reference to assist you in developing your own phrases which are most suited to your particular clients, industry, selling style and personality. Because of the hundreds of positive comments I have received regarding both the usefulness and effectiveness of these scripts, they have been collected in Appendix A for your convenience. After you have studied the book and reviewed the scripts, the spirit of the methodologies contained herein will become apparent. Most important, if employed properly and with discipline, these methods will quickly bring you to the point where you will expect and receive more referrals than you ever thought possible.

The key word in the previous sentence is "employed." When I first entered the sales profession I had the opportunity to attend many seminars, conferences and conventions where sales professionals gathered to share ideas. During my first few months I was told by a colleague that the time spent at these meetings would be worthwhile as long as I was able to leave with one good idea. As the months passed and my earnings grew, I became astonished to learn of the great number of salespeople who attended these meetings with the hope of finding the new technique that would provide them with the boost they needed to bring them to the next level of success. I wasn't puzzled by their hunger for knowledge; I am also constantly striving for professional growth. I was, however, disappointed to learn that most of these salespeople went from seminar to seminar, conference to conference, and convention to convention making very little progress in improving their income. I soon became aware of the cause of this lack of progress. Almost everyone was leaving the meeting with at least one good idea but very few put the idea into motion. What separated the superstars from the rest was simply "doing."

I feel it is very important to mention this in the introduction to my book because my ultimate goal is to help you make more money while bringing added value to your customers. If you are reading this book simply to get an idea which will add to your knowledge, I commend you, for it has been said that knowledge is the key to success. However, if you are reading this book with the intent of employing the ideas you find of value, I congratulate you. You will soon achieve a higher level of success and enjoy all the rewards that come with it!

PART I

LAYING
THE
FOUNDATION

Let us endeavor so to live that when we come to die even the undertaker will be sorry.

- Mark Twain

Chapter One

Science
vs. Art

No matter how artful or talented you are, you must follow a specific methodology to be successful in expecting and getting quality referrals. You cannot depend solely upon your personality or upon your persuasive abilities.

It is critical to follow a disciplined and organized approach to getting referrals. Otherwise you will find yourself forever stuck in the endless quagmire of cold calling, expensive advertising or direct mail marketing. Both are yielding lower and lower responses.

As you will soon learn in Chapter Five, the possibilities of generating profitable sales leads through traditional prospecting techniques are rapidly declining while their costs continue to accelerate. Salespeople and businesses who understand the phenomenal value of referrals that can be provided to them by their existing client base and who have designed a specific referral generation program for their company do not experience the expense and inefficiency associated with traditional prospecting methods. To be successful at the art of gathering referrals, you must first master the science.

When Michael Jordan made one of his amazing spin moves to the basket and finished off the play with a phenomenal slam dunk, his dazzling artistry became apparent. But oftentimes we do not consider what took place behind the scenes that made this great work of art a reality. The pick set by Scottie Pippen, the clear-out by Horace Grant, and the low post screen executed by Bill Cartwright, all contributed to Michael Jordan's masterful play. Basketball fans know that as spectacular as Michael Jordan was from day one in the National Basketball Association, it took seven years before the Chicago Bulls won the NBA championship. The artful talent was there, but talent alone was not enough to secure the ultimate victory. It took the addition and growth of other skilled players, and a coach who could blend them into a system that could function effectively. The Chicago Bulls performed surgery on their opponents. Their methods were precise and their work was science. They won the NBA championship three years in a row.

The defense of the 1992 Dallas Cowboys provides us with another example of methodology being more important than individual talent. The defense of the 1992 Cowboys was number one in the National Football League, yet not one defensive player was selected to the Pro Bowl. Individual talent was not their key to success. The coach's ability to make the best use of the skills available to him, combined with the players' ability to properly execute the plan, made their defense number one in the league. As of the printing of this book the Dallas Cowboys have won the Super Bowl two years in a row.

There are many parallels between these two sports analogies and the effective gathering of quality referrals. Of course, in both of the examples the players had talents and skills that were necessary in order for them to be successful in attaining their goals. But it was the combination of their talents and the coaches' game plans that propelled them to the top of their sport. Likewise, all top salespeople possess individual talents that they apply effectively during the sale of their product or service. They are able to apply their talents because they have been taught specific methods for gathering information about their prospects' needs, desires and goals, and have been schooled in how to present the product or service that will most effectively fill those needs. Different circumstances call for different tactics.

Unfortunately, salespeople often take their success for granted and attribute it to their individual talents, forgetting the hard work it took to learn the methods that they apply day in and day out when they are active in the selling process. So few people are able to prospect solely by referrals because salespeople, in general, have not been taught the in-depth approach required to develop a strong referral gathering system.

If you attempt to prospect using only your raw talents, you will find yourself discouraged and reverting to your old ways of doing business, while accepting as fact that it is nearly impossible to work solely on referrals. This is why it is important to study the specific methodologies and principles contained in this book. These methods, blended in harmony with your own natural selling style, will allow you to establish a referral generation program which will put an end to your prospecting problems.

At a recent company sponsored sales conference, one of my associates and I were approached by a very successful salesman who had been in sales for over twenty years. He had noticed that I was among the top five salespeople in the country and congratulated me on a year well done. He told me that he knew I was really hustling, making many calls, and burning the midnight oil. He said that if I would hang in there for six more years, I would not have to work so hard. He mentioned that once I established a good reputation with my clients, they would start referring people to me and my prospecting would be simplified. I told the gentleman that I appreciated his comments, and indeed I would be looking forward to the next six years passing quickly. As he walked away I looked at my associate and smiled as we exchanged "high fives." If he only knew, I had been working on referrals from day one. Six years from now, I hope to retire.

You may be curious as to what prompted me to write a book on a subject of such a simple nature. I have been very successful in sales and owe all of my success to my ability to gather quality referrals. My profession is in the fields of insurance and investments. Although, at the writing of this book, I have only been in this business for a little less than five years, I have managed to make enough sales to earn the recognition of being among the top producers for one of the largest insurance companies in America. I was a Marine for the eleven years preceding my entry into this business and I had no sales experience whatsoever. Although the Marine Corps did not teach me any sales techniques, I learned many lessons and developed skills which prepared me for a successful career in sales. Loyalty, integrity and the commitment to a disciplined approach in accomplishing any mission is mandatory for a successful career in the Marine Corps. The battalions in which I was a member participated in exercise after exercise, maneuver after maneuver, and operation after operation, striving to improve upon their combat efficiency by growing in both character and experience with each lesson learned.

When I entered the sales profession it seemed natural for me to apply, in my new career, the methodical disciplined approach that the Marine Corps utilized so effectively. This is why my referral system has been developed into a science. It is comprised of many small activities (or units) which individually are very simple to execute. Many sales professionals make use of one or two pieces of the referral generating process. But, just as it would be unthinkable for a Marine officer to send his or her battalion into combat without making the most effective use of all available resources, it is also unthinkable to attempt to get referrals without making effective use of all required elements of the referral generation process. The process outlined in this book must be employed with integrity and executed with commitment in a specific disciplined manner.

My peers, many of whom have dozens of years of experience over me, have been fascinated by my ability to prospect solely through referrals. Associates from Colorado, Florida, South Carolina, Pennsylvania,

North Dakota, Virginia and Minnesota have visited my agency for several days at a time in order to learn my referral methods. I have been more than happy to share my knowledge as they have been just as unselfish in teaching me the specifics of handling many complicated cases. The biggest problem I had during these three- or four-day meetings was describing all of the many facets that intertwined in the make-up of my referral system. To discuss my methods off the top of my head became rather difficult. I had never taken the time to organize the many important aspects of my system in a way that would make it easy for others to understand.

I have been asked to give seminars to businesses and other sales professionals about the methods I use to get referrals. This sincere interest of others in my profession, combined with my strong belief that this referral system can be easily learned and adapted into anyone's sales technique, has prompted me to put my system into writing.

Any salesperson knows that people use different selling styles. No matter what business you are in, you have certainly encountered salespeople who seem to have a natural talent for their job. Important questions need to be answered. Can this system be adapted to other people's personalities or is my success in getting referrals primarily due to certain personality characteristics? Is my success in gathering referrals an art which is dependent upon talent, or is it a science based on a methodology which can be easily duplicated? On the surface, if someone were to watch me during various points of contact with my clients, it may seem as if it is an art. This is because I have practiced each specific technique to the point where it has become second nature. As I have developed my scripts I have evaluated the reactions of my prospects and clients, being ever so sensitive to their emotions. The scripts in this book are client-tested and when utilized in conjunction with the other service-related techniques contained herein are proven to be effective in allowing you to generate large numbers of first class referrals.

The work of creating this system has been completed. Your job simply lies in the implementation and execution of the technique. Jim Rohn, in his motivational series of tapes, <u>Take Charge of Your Life</u>, makes a statement that we should all take to heart:

"Discipline weighs ounces...regret weighs tons."

I challenge all of my readers to be disciplined in the study of referral science. You will soon learn that the methodology involved is planned, precise and simple.

Chapter Two

Why Referrals?

During the initial drafts of this book a colleague asked me why I developed a prospecting system so different from what is being practiced by most salespeople in our business. He found it curious that someone with so little experience would begin in a way very different from the conventional prospecting methods which are currently being taught by most major corporations. This chapter has been written solely for the purpose of helping the reader understand why I could not prospect using the techniques that are taught by those in my industry. It comes down to some personal experiences which affected my life during my younger days.

The first twelve years of my life were pretty typical. I was an A/B student. I loved to go exploring in the woods behind my house and played a lot of street hockey and football in Peabody, Massachusetts. My life drastically changed in August of 1972. My mother, sister and I drove home from a weekend at Cape Cod, only to find my father dead. He had committed suicide by carbon monoxide poisoning.

I never really knew my dad. If he was not at work in Boston, he was working in the basement office of our house. In fact, we played catch with a baseball only a couple of times. He would become very frustrated when I threw the ball over his head or too far to the left or right. No matter how hard he tried, he could not get me to throw the ball straight. I was not much of an athlete at that time.

As I walked around our two-car garage which was still filled with exhaust fumes, I was amazed at the precision my father, "Ziggy," took to perform his final act. There was a fifty-five gallon drum sitting next to the 1970 Plymouth Fury III; a rubber hose led from it to the gas tank. There were wet towels rolled up (rat-tailed) and stuffed wherever light or air could penetrate: around the windows, under the garage door, on the side of the door where the rollers to the garage doors were, and underneath the door leading into our home. Ziggy was a frugal man. He lay in the front seat wearing only his underwear. He always took pride in his clothes; I guess he did not want to ruin a decent suit.

There were bricks both underneath and on top of the gas pedal so the engine would idle at the right speed. He had evidently gone to sleep reading the final company newsletter he had edited. It was not until several years later that I came to understand what a perfectionist my father was. He was nearly perfect in everything he did. His only imperfection was his inability to recognize that so many people truly cared for him. This perfectionist attitude has certainly affected part of my outlook on life and was instrumental in the design and implementation of my referral system.

Shortly after my father's death, my mother encouraged me to join a local chapter of the Order of DeMolay. DeMolay is a Masonic organization for young adults. She did this in order to help me develop some new friendships. Since my father's death, I had become very withdrawn and had no friends in our new neighborhood. It was always important to me as a child to be well-liked. I was always very careful not to offend anyone at school. Yet, since I was very thin and scrawny, I was an easy target for the school bullies. My mother felt that DeMolay would be a good outlet.

I soon became elected the Master Counselor of our chapter. As Master Counselor, I was in charge of organizing our annual fudge drive. Each of our members was tasked with selling ten cases of fudge. There were thirty-six boxes in each case. Each box contained one pound of chocolate, chocolate walnut or penuche fudge. This meant that each of us had to sell three-hundred-sixty boxes at a dollar per box. My fear of rejection overcame me. I could not knock on doors and offer people this fudge; there was a good chance that I would bother them, irritate them, or get a door slammed in my face.

Rejection may have killed my father; I would not let it kill me. My two years of allowance was then mobilized. I was the proud owner of three-hundred-sixty pounds of fudge. Six months later I was no longer a scrawny little kid, although I had developed a strong case of acne. You can't win them all.

The months following my father's death became very difficult for my mother. People who had been friends for many years soon drifted apart from mom. My mother had no interest in meeting another man and was, of course, not invited out to dine with other couples. She soon became very self-conscious, blaming herself for what she felt to be rejection. Her fears soon developed into paranoia and mental illness and, upon her hospitalization, my adopted sister and I were separated and sent to foster homes.

After several years in foster homes I dropped out of Gloucester High School in Massachusetts and climbed aboard a moped with a young lady. We were both sixteen and had decided to get jobs at Walt Disney World. Moped travel on Interstate 95 and U.S. Highway 301 was a sore proposition and by the time we got to Virginia my travelling companion decided to bail. She hitched a ride with the local sheriff back to Massachusetts and I continued on my journey to the "Sunshine State."

Upon my arrival in Florida, I got a job at a nursery digging up trees. I slept in my "Camel" pup tent hidden in the woods off of Interstate 4 until I saved enough money to be able to share an apartment. After three months, I got my dream job at Disney World flipping hamburgers at the Pinocchio Village House. A transfer sent me to Space Mountain where I met a Staff Sergeant in the Marine Corps Reserve. One look at his "dress blues" was all I needed. I was off to Parris Island, the land that God forgot.

My Marine Corps career got off to a slow start but then accelerated into a positive experience after meeting Lt. Col. Raymond E. Porter, USMC, in Okinawa, Japan. He taught me the true meaning of commitment, discipline and loyalty. Within three years he had helped me to generate a tremendous change in my attitude toward life and I soon found myself as a Staff Sergeant attending the University of Florida. I graduated Phi Beta Kappa and was commissioned as a Second Lieutenant.

Six months later, following the removal of two discs from my back, I was back on the street, dejected and with a marriage gone sour. I had also just learned that my sister had acquired the AIDS virus (she was a heroin addict and prostitute) and was in a New York State penitentiary. She had attempted to sell drugs to a DEA agent.

Since I was a child, I have been forced to endure the compounding effects of rejection. I suppose many people become thick-skinned and are able to cope even better as their experiences mount. These events had the opposite effect on me. I have become thin-skinned and not only do I fear further rejection, but I am very sensitive to the feelings and emotions of others. I guess once you've tasted enough pain, you begin to suffer when you sense pain in others. The memories of rejection I lived with, both in school and with my father, combined with the "spurning" experienced by each member of my family, have never left me.

The referral system I created is precise and simple to follow. I do not have to call upon people who would be irritated by my call. I cannot and will not make cold calls.

Chapter Three

Types of Referrals

Now that I had decided not to make cold calls, what could I do? Much had been written and many studies had been done detailing the other prospecting options available. Some options considered were: sending letters to different classes of prospective clients, giving free seminars to various groups and organizations, or simply knocking on doors and introducing myself.

Although many sales professionals find these options rewarding, there is no question that the time and effort used to pursue them are quite consuming and emotionally draining. There is also no question that working by referrals is the most effective and efficient way of expanding a business or organization.

We have used the word "referral" many times. It is important to understand both what a referral is and what it is not. A referral is a person or business recommended to you, by someone who feels that this person or business could benefit from you, your

product, or your services. A referral may not neces-
sarily be an automatic sale. Great care must be taken
in gathering information about the referral and
taking the right approach both in the timing and the
method by which the referral is contacted before,
during and after the sale.

The last thing you want to do is to say something
or engage in an activity that may irritate your
referred prospect. Any contact you have with the
referral will more than likely be related back to its
source. It is vital that any feedback is positive,
otherwise, your source for referrals will terminate.

There are three different types of referrals. It is up
to you to classify each referral into its appropriate
type by interpreting the available information. All
referrals can be classified into one of the following
types:

1.) **Cold Referral:** You are given the prospect's
name but are not allowed to make reference
to the referring person.

2.) **Warm Referral:** You are given the prospect's
name and are allowed to use the referring
person as a reference. You are provided with
no specific information regarding the
prospect's needs, desires or goals.

3.) **Hot Referral:** You are given the prospect's
name and are allowed to use the referring
person as a reference. You are also provided
with specific information regarding the
prospect's needs, desires or goals.

It is very important that each referral be placed in one of these three categories. As you will learn in Chapter Eight there is a specific way for approaching each type of referral. If a referral is not properly categorized it is very possible that a mistake could be made during the initial contact with the prospect which could jeopardize your effectiveness in both securing an appointment and getting quality referrals.

Your major focus should be on getting enough information concerning each referral's specific needs, desires and goals to upgrade all referrals into hot ones. In Chapter Twelve, you will learn how to enhance the quality of your referrals. The following are examples of cold, warm and hot referrals given to you by a client during an actual appointment:

Cold: "Try calling Ray and Dorothy Smith. They live in 'The Pines,' are in their early thirties and have two young children. Ray doesn't like people giving out his name so I'd rather you not tell him that I gave you his name."

Warm: "Try calling Ray and Dorothy Smith. They live in 'The Pines,' are in their early thirties, and have two young children. They may be interested in chatting with you. You can mention my name."

Hot: "Try calling Ray and Dorothy Smith. They live in 'The Pines,' are in their early thirties, and have two young children. I <u>know</u> they've been looking for information on your product. They would probably appreciate hearing from you."

Developing hot referrals should be the primary objective of everyone's prospecting campaign. Transforming cold or warm referrals into hot referrals will be discussed in detail later in this book. Quality relationships developed between salespeople and their clients during the entire sales process will determine the types of referrals they acquire.

We call this continuous contact with clients the Referral Cycle. We will soon learn about the Referral Cycle, but first it is important that we understand the attitudes of corporations, salespeople, and clients concerning referrals.

Chapter Four

Understanding Attitudes

In this chapter we will explore the attitudes of the three major players that have an effect on our ability to get referrals. These players are the corporations that produce the products and train our nation's sales force, the salespeople who market and distribute the products of the corporations, and the clients who utilize these products or services.

Corporations spend millions of dollars training their sales forces in product knowledge and ways of overcoming objections to the sale. These companies perform extensive research into the best approaches to selling their products or services. Most of our country's salespeople are taught step-by-step presentations designed to capture the emotions, trust and ultimately the customer's dollar. Corporations often develop sales presentations that ensure that all objections have been identified, addressed and overcome before the salesperson attempts to close the sale. Product sales techniques are designed to keep the salespeople from having to become defensive during the closing process. Indeed, the selling process is a science.

As we discussed in Chapter One, getting referrals is also a science. Unfortunately, most corporations do not invest enough of their resources toward training their salespeople in the specific methods required to effectively secure sufficient numbers of quality referrals. I have spoken with many salespeople in many industries who are not successful in getting referrals. They have been told that all they have to do is ask. It is not enough to just ask a prospect or client to provide you with referrals. Of course it is necessary to ask, but anyone who has tried knows that it is not that simple. If it were, there would be no need for this book.

Most salespeople do not ask for referrals. Why? Fear of rejection? They do not know how? Fear of jeopardizing the sale? They do not think it will work? Or is it simply because salespeople feel uncomfortable asking for referrals? Wouldn't these fears be the same emotions salespeople would have if they tried to sell their product without knowledge of the best approach or without the proper answers to objections?

Let's take a moment to put ourselves in the position of salespeople who are ill prepared to present their product or service. Let's say you are an automobile salesperson. You know the names of the eight models available for you to sell, but are not quite certain what size engine is standard with each car. You know that each automobile is equipped with a radio but are unfamiliar with the various option packages that are available. Of course you know that each car has four wheels but you haven't taken the time to learn which models have front wheel or rear wheel drive. You don't know the horsepower of the engines.

Or maybe you are a real estate broker showing someone a home with which you haven't taken the time to become familiar. You arrive at the site at the same time as your potential buyers. You know the price of the home but are not quite certain of the square footage. You know the property includes a backyard but are unfamiliar with the boundaries. You know the home has a heating and air conditioning system but are not sure of the capacity. Or maybe you sell life insurance, but you don't know the difference between whole life and universal life. Or you sell mutual funds but are unclear of the difference between international and overseas funds.

The fact is that good salespeople would never put themselves in any of these positions. You know your products better than anyone, period. Now think of the time and effort you invested in developing your knowledge. Try and remember the effort you expended in developing your sales technique. In fact, you are a **master** salesperson.

The reason you don't experience the fears discussed previously is because you are confident of both your product knowledge and salesmanship. You know that the car is equipped with a 3 liter, 24 valve, 270 horsepower V6 transverse midship-engine, has rear wheel drive, and comes standard with a Bose AM/FM stereo with a CD player. You know that the home you are about to show has 2,740 square feet of living space, is equipped with a 3 ton capacity gas heating and cooling system with a SEER rating of 14, and rests on 1 1/4 acres of land that includes a grove of hickory trees. You not only know the difference between whole life and universal life but also the historical development of the many types of policies available. Whether you sell mutual funds, computers, software or medical supplies, your knowledge of both your product and industry are superb. You have overcome the emotional roadblocks to success by becoming a master of product selling.

In order to overcome these obstacles when attempting to get referrals you must also become a master of prospecting. Salespeople are trained to deal with these fears when selling their product or service. We will soon learn how to overcome these fears when making the sale for referrals.

We have discussed the fact that most corporations have done very little training on effective referral gathering techniques. Therefore, it follows that most salespeople are not adequately prepared to effectively take full advantage of the referral process. This book will teach the science of expecting referrals, but before we learn how to get referrals and how to enhance their potential, we must first understand our clients' attitudes toward salespeople.

A brief analysis of the evolution of sales practices during this century will help us put our clients' attitudes into perspective. I hope some day to make an in-depth study of the changing psychology of sales in America during the Twentieth Century. For now, a short summary will suffice and should help you realize the growing pressures our prospects have had to tolerate.

During the first half of this century, American society was made up of many small, self-sufficient communities. Entire families were usually located within a mile of each other, and oftentimes several generations lived together as a family unit. The milkman did not simply sell milk; he was also a friend. The owner of the service station not only fixed your automobile but also pumped your gas, checked your oil, washed your windows, and even checked the air pressure in your tires. The people you did business with were your friends. They had to be your friends to stay in business. Communities were so small that if business owners or salespeople ever mistreated a customer the word would spread quickly and they would soon be forced to take down their shingle. Salespeople counted on frequent personal contacts to be exposed to the community and to increase public awareness of their product or service.

Most salespeople who specialized in a particular product or service such as life insurance or Fuller Brushes had to travel from one community to another in order to make a living. It was imperative that they developed strong relationships with each individual in the community so that they could maintain a strong foothold in that area. Each time they returned to that community they would depend upon referrals from existing clients in order to allow their business to grow. As you will learn, this art of referral generation was soon lost.

During the 1960s America underwent some of the most radical changes she had experienced in quite some time. A cultural revolution, the Vietnam War on our televisions, the Civil Rights Movement, drugs, rock and roll, assassinations, manned space flight, and the Iron Curtain are but a few of the events that contributed to the fragmentation of America. Cohesion within communities began to break up and it became more difficult for salespeople to work with groups of individuals who shared common values. It also became less necessary for salespeople to maintain close relationships with their clients, since it was unlikely that the word would travel quickly through the grapevine. Slowly, salespeople began to lose touch with the qualities that previously made them so effective in getting referrals.

As a result of the fragmentation that occurred in the previous decade, the 1970s brought about the evolution of less personal prospecting techniques. Junk mail became a household word. Every few months you could be assured of receiving a telephone call from a salesperson who wanted to sell you something. The successful salespeople of the first half of the century were beginning to retire and a new breed of go-getters was developing new prospecting techniques.

The 1980s witnessed the birth of the personal computer, and with it, came the "Age of Information." One of the most common methods of prospecting was to purchase long lists of names that fit the demographics that were being targeted. Each list was created from personal data such as income, sex, race, occupation, age, marital status, affiliations or home address. Salespeople were taught to contact as many of these prospects as possible in the shortest amount of time. They were taught that success in sales was purely a numbers game. Although it was effective, salespeople slipped further and further away from the pulse of society. Meanwhile, more of the old-timers retired.

Here we are in the 1990s. Believe it or not, many cold calls are now performed by machines. Non-profit organizations hire telemarketers to solicit donations. Not only have many salespeople become desensitized to the feelings of the public, but the public has also become desensitized to the feelings of salespeople. The high-tech approaches used by many salespeople have left the public cold. Most people will not think twice about rudely hanging up during a telephone solicitation. Yet, the cold-callers (or their computers) keep dialing. The public is angry! It is time to return to the basics! It is time to resurrect the referral process.

I hope this brief history helps you put into perspective some of the difficulties our prospects have had to endure. I am positive that you have experienced both sides of this dilemma. Now that we understand a little bit of the history which has helped to shape the attitudes of our clients, we must explore our clients' attitudes toward giving referrals.

It must be understood that if clients never had objections to giving referrals there would be no problem in getting them. A salesperson could simply ask for referrals and live happily ever after. Unfortunately, this is not the case. Without a well-designed, systematic referral gathering technique, it is nearly impossible to be successful in sales while working on a referral-only basis. Following are some of the major reasons why some clients may not wish to give referrals:

1. Clients are afraid of upsetting friends and relatives.
2. Clients feel finances are personal in nature.
3. Clients do not want friends to think they're being talked about.
4. Clients tend to qualify their friends by income or class.
5. Clients, in general, look down upon sales-people.
6. Clients may believe in the product but not in the salesperson.
7. Clients fear the salesperson may not be around years down the road.
8. Clients do not feel they can benefit from giving the salesperson referrals.
9. Clients may not know anyone to refer.

It is absolutely essential that these objections be both addressed and overcome before asking for referrals. The task of answering objections should begin during the initial contact with a potential client and continue throughout the entire referral cycle. In Appendix B, we will discuss each of these objections in detail and provide you with the methods by which you can overcome them when they materialize, if they have not yet been diffused. By the time you are ready to ask for referrals, all possible objections must be identified and addressed. Product sales tech-niques are designed to keep salespeople from becom-ing defensive during the closing process. Consumers do not buy from defensive salespeople! Likewise, when it comes time to ask for referrals, if salespeople are placed on the defensive they will, most of the time, back down and retreat in order to save the sale.

Above, we listed nine reasons why clients may be reluctant to give referrals. Read over this list and try to put yourself in the position of your client. Ask yourself if you feel comfortable giving referrals to a salesperson. If you do not, ask why.

Oftentimes it is easy for us to measure our own personal feelings. It is very difficult, however, to come to grips with and understand the emotions of others. In Chapter Two of this book I spoke briefly of the reasons why I developed my referral system. Because of the pain, discomfort and rejection I experienced in my younger years, I became very sensitive to the pain, discomfort and rejection experienced by others. In order to collect referrals effectively, a salesperson must be sensitive to a prospect's feelings.

Fear, anxiety, and apprehension must be soothed before you can expect referrals. These are the same emotions that are allayed during the process of selling the product. This is a classic example of a sale within the sale. While the product is being presented in the most perfect light, a parallel referral sale must be nurtured beginning from the time of the initial contact. The referral sale receives equal importance, effort and emphasis as the product sale. This is the key to the Referral Cycle.

Chapter Five

Vanishing Possibilities

The possibilities of generating useful sales leads through modern prospecting techniques are rapidly declining. In the previous chapter, we discussed the evolution of prospecting which has helped shape the attitudes of our clients. One reason to prospect strictly through referrals is that your career will bring you greater joy and higher profits while bringing added value to your customers.

Another reason may be even more important. Soon many modern prospecting techniques such as telemarketing and mass mailings may become more regulated or even outlawed. With the growth of technology it is very likely that in the near future consumers and business owners will have the ability to filter direct mail, telemarketing, faxes or other unwanted solicitations before they ever reach the home or business. As you are probably well aware, it is becoming more and more difficult to prospect through conventional means.

This chapter serves as a reference to highlight some of the actions taken by the United States Congress and the courts. It will also inform you of various positions and statements by leaders in the telemarketing industry. Most successful entrepreneurs have the ability to position their product or service ahead of changes in the marketplace. Some of the information contained in this chapter may help you fine tune your current prospecting methodologies so you will become better positioned in the coming decade.

THE DIMINISHING EFFICIENCY OF TELEMARKETING

Of all the prospecting techniques, telemarketing (cold calls) has probably received the largest amount of criticism. Whether a non-profit organization is searching for charitable donations or a company is attempting to save consumers money on their long distance telephone service, the public is getting annoyed with the unwelcome intrusions. Because of the uproar, corporations have been forced to create telemarketing suppression files. These files contain the names and telephone numbers of citizens who have informed the sales organizations of their desire for privacy. If an individual on this list is called by a representative of the corporation, the individual has the basis to file suit against the calling company. Many state legislatures have passed laws restricting the times when their citizens can be contacted by telemarketers. Almost every state has placed severe restrictions on automatic dialing machines and it is widely believed that these machines will soon be outlawed. Because of the uproar from many "watch-dog" organizations, several associations and groups have terminated their practice of selling membership lists to telemarketing companies and corporations that purchase lists for their salespeople.

Several years ago it was not hard to call upon and speak with a corporate decision maker. However, today secretaries, office managers, and executive assistants are trained and paid to determine the specific nature of a call before allowing it to reach its intended destination. More and more business owners, executives and professionals have created filters to insulate them from unwanted sales calls. Many corporations have installed voice mail systems so that the decision makers may screen their calls to avoid wasting precious time chatting with salespeople.

The changing attitudes and activities listed above have increased the cost and reduced the efficiency of cold calling. Simply put, it takes more calls and a much greater effort to achieve the same results.

THE DIMINISHING RETURNS OF DIRECT MAIL MARKETING

Although both businesses and the public have been inundated with cold calls, the volume of these efforts is miniscule compared to the countless tons of direct mail marketing materials (junk mail) received on a daily basis. It is not uncommon for a small business owner to spend several hours a week sorting through these direct mail efforts.

Many business owners and individuals don't take the time to open their junk mail. The gurus of advertising have caught on to this and have become more creative in packaging their junk mail. Messages which seem to be hand written on the outside of envelopes, or envelopes which have the appearance of containing official business or a check made out to the addressee are commonplace. Of course, most people receiving this new wave of solicitation have come to realize the contents of these mailers and discard the packages or envelopes unopened. These actions have inevitably resulted in less exposure for the advertisers, thus lowering their response ratio. At the same time, the cost of postage has increased and is set to increase another ten percent in the near future. Also, many corporations have been forced to create mass marketing suppression files similar to those required of telemarketers.

The combined effects of direct mail marketing and telemarketing have had a definite impact upon public attitudes toward salespeople. Unfortunately, people tend to stereotype others by profession even if their methodologies differ from the norm. Salespeople in almost any industry are usually categorized as uncaring, greedy and inconsiderate. After all, who else would call upon homeowners and business owners at inconvenient times with the hope of selling a product or service?

The March, 1991 issue of *American Demographics* magazine contained a survey by the Roper organization in which families of incomes of greater than $15,000 per year responded to the question: "Is telemarketing very annoying?" Sixty-eight percent said that telemarketing was very annoying when there was a person making the call, and seventy-five percent said it was very annoying when a machine was on the other end of the line. *Telemarketing* magazine recently published a survey by Walker Research concerning consumer perceptions of telemarketing. The survey found that seventy percent of those questioned viewed telemarketing as an invasion of privacy, while sixty-nine percent thought it was an offensive way to sell. *Inc.* magazine of January, 1989, published another Roper poll showing that eighty-three percent of the public prefers not to be called, while sixty-seven percent had cut off or hung up on the most recent telemarketing effort. Though each of these surveys is a few years old, it is a safe bet to assume that perceptions haven't improved any since. Listed below are various positions and statements by individuals speaking for and against the telemarketing industry.

Miss Manners - (regarding a solicitor's complaint of rude televictims) "...you cannot reasonably expect people to separate the personal motivation of a stranger from the task he is doing. And what you are doing is rude ... many react as if a stranger has broken into the house, as indeed one has." - Judith Martin, Syndicated Columnist, 6/93

Telemarketing Leader - "If somebody is adamant that telemarketing calls are an intrusion, then the telephone itself is an intrusion into privacy and no one should have telephones." - President, Rocky Mountain Telemarketing Association

Telemarketer of the Year - "One of the other problems we've had is the amount of junk calls there are, everything from land deals to anything you can imagine you can sell over the phone...The consumer is getting fed up with this." - Mike McDonald, *TV Guide* Telemarketing Manager, honored by Target Marketing, 10/89

Direct Marketing Association Government Affairs Director - "How can we hope to change our image in the eyes of the rest of the world when we ourselves resent (junk calls) as well?" - Julie Crooker

Direct Marketing Association Senior Vice President (Telenuisance Industry Chief Lobbyist) - "...telemarketers must continually remind themselves that theirs is the most obtrusive of the advertising media." - Dick Barton, *Direct Marketing News*, 9/30/91

As you can see, this is an emotionally charged issue affecting tens of millions of Americans and only promises to grab more of the limelight as time passes. Below are four important Federal Court Rulings on the subject.

Carey vs. Brown - "Our decision reflects...the right...to be let alone in the privacy of the home. Sometimes the last citadel of the tired, the weary and the sick."

FCC vs. Pacific Foundation - "...in the privacy of the home...the individual's right to be left alone plainly outweighs the First Amendment rights of the intruder."

Rowan vs. U.S. Post Office - "...individual autonomy must survive to permit every household to exercise control over unwanted mail."

Martin vs. Struthers - "...the decision as to whether a canvasser may lawfully call on a home is with the homeowner."

These rulings, combined with the thousands of complaints sent to members of Congress, prompted the adoption into law of the "Telephone Consumer Protection Act of 1991." This Act (Public Law 102-

243) states that "Over 30,000 businesses actively telemarket goods and services, employing more than 300,000 solicitors who call more than 18 million Americans every day." The Act also reveals that in 1990, sales in the United States generated through telemarketing amounted to $435 billion. Section 2(6) further finds that "many consumers are outraged over the proliferation of intrusive nuisance calls to their homes from telemarketers." For your convenience the findings of the Act are reprinted in Appendix C of this book.

Several "watchdog" organizations have been formed in recent years to help carry the banner for consumers in the fight against telemarketers, cold callers, and junk mail solicitors. The most vocal of these, and probably the organization that has had the greatest impact in affecting state and federal laws, is Private Citizen, Inc. This Naperville, Illinois based company, founded by Robert Bulmash, distributes a directory of its members to over 1,100 telemarketing firms and list sellers warning them of a $500.00 charge should the members of Private Citizen be solicited.

The growth of these "watchdog" organizations ,along with the various court rulings, federal legislation, pending state legislation, and increased cost of cold calling and direct mail marketing, combine to strengthen the necessity for alternative prospecting methods. Without question the most effective means of prospecting is the establishment and maintenance of a referral generation system. In Part II of this book you will learn how to harness the incredible value of customer referrals.

Are you missing your most powerful prospects of all? Once you apply the concept of the parallel referral sale to your everyday dealings with clients and prospects and actively utilize the specific techniques during each phase of the Referral Cycle you will be introduced to more quality leads than you ever dreamed possible, and you will avoid ever tightening government restrictions.

PART II

THE
WHEEL
OF
FORTUNE

Confident people know that the accomplishment of any worthwhile endeavor requires commitment.

- David McNally

Chapter Six

The Referral Cycle

Getting referrals is an ongoing process. As a salesperson you must realize that every contact with a client or prospect provides you with an opportunity to promote yourself and your product or service, alleviate objections and obtain referrals.

Because salespeople are paid to sell, they are very good at using every possible opportunity to promote the value of their product or service. They are also very conscientious in taking advantage of every opportunity to answer customer objections. As we discussed in Chapter Four, you are most likely a master salesperson. You are a master because you take advantage of every opportunity to help tip the scales in your favor when selling your product. To be a master prospector, you employ the same rationale when striving to get more leads, realizing that the best leads are those that are referred to you by satisfied customers. You should constantly strive to take advantage of every opportunity to tip the prospecting scales in your favor. Each particular occasion that provides you with an opportunity to enhance your ability to get referrals is illustrated in the following diagram called the Referral Cycle.

THE REFERRAL CYCLE

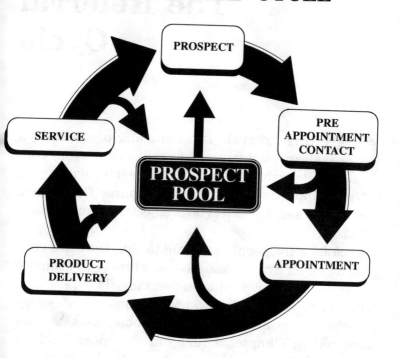

The Referral Cycle is made up of four distinct phases: Pre-Appointment Contact, Appointment, Product Delivery, and Service and Follow-Up. During each phase there are specific ideas that must be communicated to the prospect or client and specific activities that must be accomplished in order to be successful in getting referrals.

In the following chapters you will learn the specific steps that you can take during each phase of the Referral Cycle to greatly increase the willingness of your prospects and clients to provide you with quality referrals.

The Referral Cycle is a classic example of "Which came first, the chicken or the egg?" The Referral Cycle is a continuous process without beginning or end. If you have a sales presentation tonight, you can begin the Referral Cycle under the section titled "Appointment." If you are delivering a product to a client, you can start the cycle under the section titled "Product Delivery." If you are planning on making telephone calls tonight, you can begin at the "Pre-Appointment Contact" section.

Regardless of where you are in the Referral Cycle, you can begin at that point and apply the soon to be discussed techniques. You will perfect your techniques so that you will be working on every phase of the cycle simultaneously. The following chapters will explain in detail what techniques and scripts to use during each phase of the cycle to help develop your referral gathering capabilities. We will take a moment, however, to briefly introduce the Referral Cycle as a whole.

We will begin with the prospect pool. Simply put, the prospect pool is a group of names gathered from various sources. Your source may be a mailing list, telephone book, work roster or your existing clients. Eventually, your prospect pool will consist solely of referrals. From this pool you choose a prospect to contact. A new Referral Cycle has begun.

Any contact with the prospect must be geared toward presenting yourself and your product or service in such a way as to overcome any objections you could face later when asking for referrals and, of course, when making a sale. Your next step is to have contact with the prospect either face-to-face or via telephone. This is the "Pre-Appointment Contact" phase of the Referral Cycle. As we will soon discuss, much can be accomplished during this initial contact which will allow you easier access to your prospect's family members, friends or business associates. We will detail the approaches you must use in order to secure an appointment while, at the same time, setting the stage for future referral gathering opportunities. Although different salespeople utilize a broad spectrum of techniques in securing an appointment, it is important that referrals be discussed during this initial contact. Once the appointment has been scheduled, you move on to the next phase of the Referral Cycle which is "The Appointment."

The Appointment phase may be only a short meeting but in some cases may extend over a series of meetings. Regardless, the phase continues until the sale is completed. It is vital that you develop a "bond" between yourself and your prospect. It is also important that you set yourself apart, in a positive way, from all other salespeople. Once this is accomplished and your product or service satisfies the needs of your client, the sale will be made and the client will be willing to refer others to you. It is easy to forget the parallel referral sale and focus solely on the product sale. You must look long-term and consider from where your next prospect will come.

The next phase of the Referral Cycle is called "Product Delivery." During this phase we reassure our clients of our sincerity and rekindle the fires that lead to referrals. It is during this time that you must reaffirm your commitment to your clients' well-being and verify their satisfaction in the product or service that you have provided.

Once the product is delivered, the "<u>Service and Follow-Up</u>" phase begins. The Service and Follow-Up phase is the longest phase in the Referral Cycle and must not be neglected. During each of the other phases we have made promises and commitments which must be kept. The Service and Follow-Up phase provides you the opportunity to continually replenish your prospect pool with new referrals, while enhancing the referrals you have already received. In Chapter Eleven, I will give several ideas on how to improve the service you are currently offering.

Each of the coming chapters will contain a variety of scripts to help you effectively communicate your intentions to your prospects and clients. These scripts can be easily adapted to suit the particulars of the industry you represent. Most important, they provide you with a template that keeps you on the dual track to fulfilling the parallel referral sale.

Now that you have a basic understanding of the components of the Referral Cycle, we will discuss each phase of the cycle in detail.

Chapter Seven

Selecting Prospects

The prospect pool is the "holding tank" for your cold, warm, and hot referrals. Information regarding these prospects may be kept on index cards or may be managed by one of the many software programs on the market. (The pool management system is discussed in detail in Chapter Fourteen.)

As long as the ongoing referral gathering process continues, the prospect pool is replenished exponentially by referrals which have come from the four points of entry: the Pre-Appointment Contact phase, Appointment phase, Product Delivery phase, and the Service and Follow-Up phase. Choosing which new referral to contact should not be a haphazard process. The tendency would be to choose the ten hottest prospects and contact them first. This is not a good practice. It is very possible that a cold or warm referral could be the gold mine we all eagerly await. When choosing prospects to contact, an equal number of cold, warm and hot referrals should be picked

and worked simultaneously. Contact with cold and warm referrals begins the process by which they may evolve into hot referrals. Cold and warm referrals take more nurturing. Generally, over a two to six month period, these prospects will be ready to meet with you. (In Chapter Twelve we will discuss in detail the process by which the quality of your referrals can be enhanced.) Hot referrals tend to be ready to meet with you in short order.

When you begin the process of selecting the prospects to contact, you first select all the prospects to be called on that date. These are prospects whom you have previously contacted and who requested that you call them back at a later date. Typically, these are your cold and warm referrals. Once you have selected those prospects with whom you are due to follow-up, you then choose three or four new names from each of the three referral types. Generally, you should have a dozen people to call: three or four hot referrals, three or four warm referrals, three or four cold referrals and one or two follow-ups. This gives you a broad diversity of telephone calls to make and helps the telephone process become less taxing.

You should stagger these calls so that you never call two of the same referral types back to back. No one likes to get rejected four times in a row. For example, begin with a cold referral, follow with a hot one, then with a warm referral and then maybe call someone with whom you were supposed to follow-up. Repeat this process until you are satisfied with your scheduled appointments. You will soon find that your prospecting time is far more pleasant than it was in the past. Referred leads tend to be very receptive to your call.

Because your prospects are referrals, they are oftentimes hesitant to tell you that they are not interested in your products or service. It is important that you stay out of the trap of calling the same people week after week. Some people don't know how to say no and will continually put you off by asking you to call them back at a later time. During my first two years in the sales profession, it was amazing to see the telephone relationship I began to develop with prospects who didn't want to hurt my feelings by saying no. But they actually wasted a lot of my precious time by stringing me along.

This situation also occurs with people who habitually reschedule or miss appointments. Most of the time they have a very sincere excuse; however, the truth is you are not a high enough priority in their life. I finally developed a sense for knowing when to let go of these prospects. Now that you are aware that even very kind people can waste your time, you will know when to cut them loose. The best way to deal with this situation is to call these prospects and say:

"Hello Joe, this is Scott Kramnick. How are you today?... Great. The reason I'm calling is because both you and I have been so busy lately that it has been impossible for us to set up a firm time to get together. Joe, most folks would probably continue to call you week after week until you get to the point where you become irritated. Because I work strictly through referrals, I don't want you to get upset with me. If Charlie ever found out that I was bugging you, I'm sure he'd never give me any more referrals. If you could do me a favor, I'd really appreciate it. I'm going to send you a brochure outlining my services, along with my business card. When your workload lightens up would you give me a call so that we can set up a time to meet? This way the next time we talk, it will be at a time when it is convenient and comfortable for you. Is that fair enough?... Terrific. And please don't forget, if in the meanwhile you run into someone else who you feel may benefit from my services, please give me a call and let me know who they are. Thanks a lot, I look forward to hearing from you soon."

Take the time to study the script and make adjustments in it as you feel appropriate. As you begin to apply this principle to those prospects who seem to drag you on forever, you will be pleasantly surprised to find how many of them finally come to realize that your time is also valuable and maybe indeed you have a product or service that warrants further investigation. More important, when you let go of these crutches which often give you a false sense of security, you will be able to concentrate more of your time and energy on other prospects who are willing to spend their money.

The important thing to learn from this chapter is, when selecting prospects to call upon, stagger your follow-up calls with your cold, warm and hot referrals, while avoiding the tendency to focus too much of your energy on any one of these categories. The following chapter will discuss what should be said during the initial telephone or personal contact with each type of referral.

Chapter Eight

Pre-Appointment Contact

Great care must be taken during the Pre-Appointment Contact phase of the Referral Cycle. Whether the initial contact is face-to-face or via telephone, the effectiveness of your approach will be the deciding factor in determining whether or not you are given the opportunity to make a sales presentation.

Your prospects, whether they be individuals, organizations or businesses, are constantly hounded by pressing salespeople representing many different industries. Many salespeople are under pressure to produce a certain amount of business during a fixed period of time. They can often be relentless. Because most salespeople do not work strictly through referrals, they have been trained to press as hard as they can during their cold-calling process. They have been told that an objection is an opportunity to close again. In fact, I have seen many "objection sheets" that are given to salespeople with quick one-liners followed by another "close." It is not uncommon for

a prospect to have to answer "no" several times before the salesperson relinquishes. Your prospects have become desensitized to hurting the feelings of salespeople who are trying to do their job. Many prospects will hang up the phone as soon as they suspect an attempt is being made to sell them something.

You must realize that the referrals we contact, whether they be cold, warm or hot, have oftentimes been previously contacted, preyed upon and harassed by many other salespeople. This is the first negative emotion to which you must be sensitive when you contact your prospects. If, in the first several seconds, you fail to overcome their initial feelings of discomfort and intrusion, your chances of developing a relationship are slim.

Mentioning that a friend or business acquaintance of theirs recommended that you call helps alleviate some of the initial anxiety in overcoming quick objections. This is one of the reasons why working on referrals is so effective. Certainly, people are willing to listen a little bit longer if they know a person whom they trust has caused this personal contact to occur. This is why you must strive to get warm or hot referrals. Calling a cold referral is virtually the same as making a cold call. In the following sections we will discuss the type of approach to be used in dealing with each of the referral types. Do not forget that every referral must be categorized into one of the three referral types (cold, warm and hot). Each of these types is handled in a distinctly different fashion. We will illustrate three examples under each section. The professions we have chosen are financial planning, real estate, and computer sales. You should have no difficulty adapting the scripts to your particular profession.

Cold Referral - The only thing that distinguishes a cold referral from a cold call is that the client who gave you the cold referral most likely provided you with some information that your competitors do not have. In Chapter Three, we explained that a cold referral is one in which you are not allowed to make reference to the referring person's name. The key to making the best of a cold referral is to effectively utilize the information that you have been provided. This information may be very minimal such as marital status, where they live or where they work. You must prethink your initial contact approach and be prepared to soothe the referrals' discomfort with an idea that will immediately cause them to relax their guard. Once this occurs you may then begin warming up this referral. Remember your ultimate goal is an appointment. Below we highlight three examples which utilize information provided to us by the referring person. Keep in mind that we are not allowed to mention our clients' names.

In this example we are told that Ray and Dorothy Smith are married, in their early thirties, and have two young children. We are informed that they live in a residential neighborhood called "The Pines" and that Mr. and Mrs. Smith own a small hardware store. We are also told that we can not mention that our client gave us their name. We will assume the contact occurs over the telephone.

> *"Hello, is this Mr. Smith? ... My name is Scott Kramnick from Kramnick and Associates. How are you this evening? ... The reason I'm calling is because I'm working with families in 'The Pines,' helping them plan for the college education of their kids and I thought I'd give you a call to see if you would be interested in chatting about the various options available to you. Is college planning something to which you've given much thought? ..."*

OR

> *"Hello, is this Mrs. Smith? ... My name is Scott Kramnick from Kramnick Realty,. How are you today? ... The reason I'm calling is because I am working with growing families in your area, who may be interested in the possibility of moving into a larger home. I thought I'd give you a call to find out if this is something you*

have considered and, if so, I would welcome the opportunity to represent you in finding the most qualified buyer for your home. Have you given much thought to looking for a larger home? ..."

OR

"Hello, is this Mr. Smith? ... My name is Scott Kramnick from Kramnick's Komputers. How are you this afternoon? ... The reason I'm calling is because I am helping many small businesses cut inventory and labor costs by making effective use of user friendly inventory management systems. I thought I'd give you a call to find out if you are already working with a systems consultant. And, if not, I would welcome the opportunity to stop by and give you some information that you may find of great value. Is this an area to which you've given much thought? ..."

Notice how the telephone approach ended with a question that steers Mr. or Mrs. Smith into allowing us to elaborate further. If they answer the question with a "yes," we would then ask what actions, if any, they have taken to begin the college planning, home searching or inventory control process. If they answer "no," we would ask if this is something to which they feel they should begin to give some thought. In either case a dialogue has begun, and we have an opportunity to develop their interest in order to secure an appointment.

It is very important that you avoid the tendency to be too pushy when dealing with cold referrals. Although you are not revealing the name of the referring person, there is always a chance that if you irritate these prospects they may warn their friends of their bad experience. If one of those friends happens to be the referring person you can forget ever getting another referral. Of even greater consideration is the desire we should all have in making the selling experience a positive one for our consumers. A pushy salesperson may get in the door, and may even make a sale, but if the entire selling process was not pleasurable for the customer the chances for getting referrals is almost zero. Besides, we should be sensitive to the emotions of our prospects if we ever plan on developing lasting relationships.

Warm Referral - As with a cold referral it is important to effectively utilize the information that you have been provided. The only difference between a cold referral and a warm referral is that in the warm referral you are allowed to make reference to your clients as the referring people. The use of your clients' names helps to break the ice and serves to endorse you and your services. Notice the difference between the cold and warm referral approaches.

> *"Hello, is this Ray? ... Hi, Ray, my name is Scott Kramnick from Kramnick and Associates. How are you this evening? ... John and Barbara Jones are clients of mine. I met with them a couple of weeks ago and shared some ideas concerning retirement planning and college plan-*

ning. They were really excited about the services I had to offer and since I work strictly on referrals they were kind enough to mention that you might be interested in talking about college planning for your kids. What I would like to do is set up a time to chat with you and Dorothy about college planning or some of your other financial goals and show you some of the options available to help you achieve them. It's not really important to me that we do business; all I ask is if you appreciate the time we share together, if you feel that you benefit from the time we spend together, and, most important, if you respect my integrity, you would be willing to pass my name on to a friend or business associate who may also benefit from my services, just as John and Barbara did. Is that fair enough?"

OR

"Hello, is this Dorothy? ... Hi, Dorothy, my name is Scott Kramnick from Kramnick Realty. How are you today? ... John and Barbara Jones are clients of mine. I recently worked with them finding the most qualified buyer for their home and helped them choose a new home that satisfied all of their desires. They were really pleased with my service. And since I work strictly through referrals, they were kind enough to mention that at some

time you may benefit from the services I have to offer. I would like to set up a time to meet with you and Ray and leave you some information which I feel you will find of great value. It's not really important to me that we do business at this time, after all the timing may not yet be appropriate for you to consider moving. It's not really important to me that we do business; all I ask is if you appreciate the time we share together, if you feel that you benefit from the time we spend together, and, most important, if you respect my integrity, you would be willing to pass my name on to a friend or business associate who may also benefit from my services, just as John and Barbara did. Is that fair enough?"

OR

"Hello, is this Ray? ... Hi, Ray, my name is Scott Kramnick from Kramnick's Komputers. How are you this afternoon? ... John and Barbara Jones are clients of mine. I met with them last week and helped them upgrade their database management system which they found to be a great savings for their business. They were really pleased with both my product and service. And since I work primarily through referrals, they were kind enough to mention that you might be interested in learning about the value I have to offer.

I'd like to set up a time to stop by your store and share some ideas that you may find of great benefit. It's not really important to me that we do business; all I ask is if you appreciate the time we share together, if you feel that you benefit from the time we spend together, and, most important, if you respect my integrity, you would be willing to pass my name on to a friend or business associate who may also benefit from my services, just as John and Barbara did. Is that fair enough?"

Unlike the cold referral approach in which the final question leads to a barrier breaking discussion, the warm referral approach ends in a very pointed question. We are telling Ray and Dorothy that it is not important to us to make a sale. We are asking them if they feel it is reasonable, if and only if they are happy with us, that they pass our name on just as their good friends did. It is easy for Ray or Dorothy to answer "yes." We have presented our offer in a non-threatening manner which was endorsed by their friends, John and Barbara.

To say "It's not really important to me that we do business," is a very unusual statement. Consumers are not accustomed to hearing a salesperson say that it is not important to make a sale. Of course, salespeople don't make a habit of *telling* their prospects that it is of the utmost importance that the customer decides to buy. Salespeople don't say that they have to fill quotas for the month, that the closing of a deal will qualify them for a special bonus, or that their families will starve if they don't soon make a sale. But anyone who has ever been one-on-one with a salesperson certainly senses the pressure, and the pressure is on both the salesperson and the prospect. By telling the prospect that your focus lies in building a relationship which will eventually lead to referrals, much of the pressure is relieved. You have allayed their fears of doing business with a pushy salesperson who will do anything to get a sale.

Today's consumers seek relationships with people they can trust. When you make a strong case that your business is dependent on getting referrals, the prospect knows that the burden is on the salesperson to provide a quality product with quality service. Otherwise, the referrals will cease. This is the crux of expecting referrals. Relationships. Period. We are given an opportunity to present our product for sale. The Referral Cycle will continue.

Hot Referral - What distinguishes a hot referral from a warm referral is that with a hot referral you are told about a specific need, desire or goal that your prospects wish to address. Hot referrals are usually provided to you by individuals who are very close to them. Appointments with hot referrals are the easiest to secure, as long as the specific need mentioned by the referring people is the main point of discussion during the initial conversation with your prospects. You should never discuss other services that you offer during the initial contact with hot referrals unless you are asked to do so. There will be plenty of time in the future to educate the prospect about the many services you provide. Their current needs are what they are most concerned with and should be your only focus. It is easy to fall into the trap of becoming too excited when you know that prospects are receptive to an idea. You should not allow this excitement to overtake you and cause you to feel that they will be just as receptive to the other services you offer. To present these prospects with a laundry list of services may be interpreted as trivializing their immediate needs and may cause you to appear unconcerned about their true needs. Remember the ultimate goal is to secure the appointment. Once you have the appointment and earn their trust, they will be far more receptive to hearing about the other ways in which they can benefit from your services.

In the following example, our clients, John and Barbara, have told us that during a recent game of bridge, their friends, Ray and Dorothy, discussed their worries about having the financial ability to send their kids to college. (Of course, depending upon the nature of the business you did with John and Barbara, their friends may have discussed their desire to start a college plan for their kids, to move into a larger home or their need to upgrade their antiquated business computer system.) Notice the conversation is directed specifically towards their needs.

"Hello, is this Ray? ... Hi, Ray, this is Scott Kramnick from Kramnick and Associates. How are you doing this evening? ... The reason I'm calling is because John and Barbara, besides being half-way decent bridge players, are clients of mine. Since I work strictly on referrals they were kind enough to mention that you had

expressed an interest in preparing for your children's college education. What I would like to do is set up a time to meet with you and Dorothy and discuss the different options available. What would be a good time for us to get together?"

OR

"Hello, is this Dorothy? ...Hi, Dorothy, this is Scott Kramnick from Kramnick Realty. How are you doing today? ... The reason I'm calling is because John and Barbara, besides being half-way decent bridge players, are clients of mine. Since I work strictly on referrals they were kind enough to mention that you are considering moving into a larger home. What I would like to do is set up a time to meet with you and Ray to discuss the best way to find a qualified buyer for your current home while we search for a new home that fulfills your expectations. What would be a good time for us to get together?"

OR

"Hello, is this Ray? ... Hi, Ray, this is Scott Kramnick from Kramnick's Komputers. How are you doing today? ... The reason I'm calling is because John and Barbara, besides being half-way decent bridge players, are clients of mine. Since I work strictly on referrals they

> *were kind enough to mention that you*
> *have considered upgrading your company's*
> *computer system. What I would like to do*
> *is set up a time to meet with you to discuss*
> *the various hardware and software prod-*
> *ucts that you may find valuable in helping*
> *you achieve your business goals. What*
> *would be a good time for us to get*
> *together?"*

As you can see, conversation with hot referrals requires the least amount of psychology. We were told that Ray and Dorothy had a definite need that they wanted to address. We focused on that need while mentioning its source and the fact that we work strictly on referrals. There was no need to discuss anything further except the date and time of our meeting.

The above examples outline the way in which each type of referral must initially be approached. Whether the initial contact is face-to-face or over the telephone, it is important that you do not deviate from the formats we have discussed. This first contact with your prospect must be a pleasant experience. In the chapter "Understanding Attitudes," we listed several reasons why clients are often hesitant about giving referrals. For the most part, they fear that their friends may have an unpleasant experience and will hold them accountable for it. The best way to overcome this concern is to make sure your prospects have a positive encounter with you. Remember where you got the prospects' names. If this contact is not positive, the experience will certainly be relayed back to your clients and you can forget about ever getting any more referrals from them. If the experience turns out to be rewarding, not only will you gain new clients, but they will be willing to pass your name on to their friends. The clients who referred you to them will certainly learn of this beneficial contact. It will not take long for the referrals to come your way.

You noticed that during the telephone call to the warm and hot referrals, I mentioned that I work "strictly on referrals." This is very important. It tells your prospects that they are receiving special attention because only by referral would you be contacting them. Also, in each of these examples, I did not stop talking until I had finished my entire presentation. This is also very important. Everything you have to say must be presented before you make the request for the appointment.

A disciplined, consistent approach will always win over an emotional, wavering discussion. Take the time to compare the above conversations and note the similarities and differences between them. Use these approaches effectively and you will have more selling opportunities. In the following chapter we will learn how these selling opportunities will lead to more referrals.

Chapter Nine

The Appointment

Depending upon the particular industry you represent, the situation in which you present your product or service for sale may be called by a variety of names. It could be a meeting, appointment, interview or presentation. Hereafter, we will refer to it as the appointment.

During the appointment you have the greatest opportunity to influence your prospect. It is important to understand that your prospect will scrutinize everything you say and do, whether it be through words, expressions or body language. Because of this, the company for whom you are selling the product or service has spared no expense in designing a presentation that allows both you and your product or service to be viewed in the best possible light.

During this presentation you also must be conscious of presenting your desire to get referrals. We call this the *parallel referral sale*. Equal emphasis must be given to both the product sale and the referral sale.

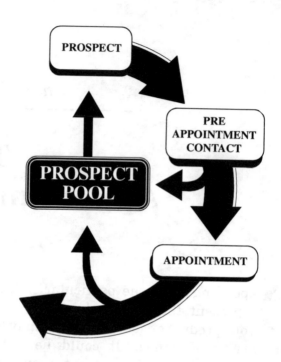

Some salespeople fear that asking for referrals shows a sign of weakness to the prospect. I have spoken with many salespeople who felt that asking for referrals might give their prospects the impression that there is a lack of buying interest in the product. This is not true. More than anything, a prospect respects honesty and integrity. A strong consistent referral presentation throughout the sales process shows your potential clients that you are a genuine individual whom they have the opportunity to help. They know you will benefit if they buy your product or service. Presenting a request for referrals relieves some of the pressure and tension created by the product sales presentation. It also shows your clients that you are seeking a two-way relationship which will be long-lasting. They will continually benefit from your product or service. As long as this product or service and the relationship with your clients are of high quality, you will continually benefit from their referrals.

The Appointment phase of the Referral Cycle actually begins when you sit down with your prospects for the purpose of making a sales presentation. As comfortably as possible, you should make a conscious effort to mention the referring person. This may be a remark as simple as:

> *"Jason told me that you liked to golf. Did you get a chance to get out this week?"*
>
> or
>
> *"Elizabeth mentioned that you like to garden. Did the last frost we had affect your plants at all?"*

This initial contact plants the seed for the beginning of the referral sale. During the next ten or fifteen minutes there should be no discussion about the product or service being offered. This time is best used to build rapport and help break down any barriers between the prospects and their perception of you as a salesperson. To accelerate this process you should mention the referring person as often as possible. It is easy to tell when the barriers begin to come down. The walls of resistance have fallen when you begin to feel comfortable with your prospects. If you do not feel comfortable with your prospects, they certainly do not feel comfortable with you.

Once you establish rapport, you should take a

moment to explain to your prospects what will occur during the time you will be together. It doesn't matter what product or service you are selling; this approach should be used regardless.

Every appointment should be divided into three parts. During the first part you should discuss yourself, including the work you do in the community, your personal successes, a little bit about your background and the service you provide to your clients. The second part of the appointment should consist of gathering information concerning the prospects' needs, desires and goals. The third part of the appointment should provide them with the information to help them achieve their objectives. You should be forthright in telling your prospects what is to come. After you establish rapport, use a simple introduction such as the following.

> *"What I'd like to do with you tonight is basically three things. First, I'd like to tell you a little bit about myself and my company so you will feel comfortable with whom you are doing business. Second, I'd like to hear about you so I feel comfortable in understanding exactly what your needs, desires and goals are. Then third, we will discuss the different options available to help you achieve your objectives. Is that fair enough?"*

Not only does this introduction serve to help you organize your appointment but it also forces you to spend some time selling yourself. During the first part of the appointment you will have several opportunities to credit your success to the many clients whom you serve and to their generosity in providing you with referrals. People rarely give referrals because of their belief in your product. Usually they will only give referrals because of their belief in you.

This first part of the appointment is important in earning the trust of your clients. It also makes sure they are comfortable with the fact that you work strictly through referrals. I cannot overemphasize the importance of the first part of the appointment. I will typically spend fifteen to twenty minutes on this phase.

The ironic fact is that if you take sufficient time to tactfully build yourself up, the odds are increased that you will make a sale. Most people like to be a part of another's success and will be willing to help that person succeed further. Your prospects must be made to feel that they are an integral part of the team. This is also a good time to explain the other services you provide such as birthday cards, thank-you cards, newsletters, annual follow-ups, seminars, and any other services.

It is important that you tell your prospects that the reason you provide these services is not because you are a good person or a good Christian. You must tell them that you provide these services because you work strictly on referrals and that when you take good care of your clients, they take good care of you. I always tell my prospects that I do everything possible to provide them with the best service because it makes good business sense. You can do this with the following remarks.

> *"If I take good care of you, then I hope you will be willing to pass my name on to other people who would appreciate the same honesty and integrity I have extended to you. I don't do this because I'm a good guy, or because I'm a good Christian; I do it because it makes good business sense. If I take care of you, you'll take care of me."*

You must realize that your prospects have been promised excellent service many times in the past. Unfortunately, they have rarely been benefactors of the same. As the years have passed and your prospects have fallen victims to more and more empty promises, they have come to accept that hearing these empty promises is part of the buying process. What will separate you from your competition is not only standing by your word but also informing your prospects of your motives. Convincing your prospects that you have made referral gathering a major focus of your business not only strengthens your relationships with them but also lends support to your promise of outstanding service. If your prospects are convinced that you are committed to getting referrals, they will be equally convinced that you are committed to providing the best possible service. After all, how could you ever expect referrals from an unhappy customer? Here are a couple of other scripts to help you enrich this point:

> *"I am honored to have the opportunity to meet with you today. I am offering you more than a product or service. I am offering you a relationship which I am*

sure will continue to grow through the years."

OR

"My success and the success of my business is totally dependent upon getting quality referrals from my clients. I realize that you will introduce me to your friends, family and business associates only if the quality and integrity of the service I provide surpasses that to which you've grown accustomed. This I pledge."

Once you are satisfied that your prospect has no doubt about your intentions, move into the second phase of the appointment. As discussed previously, this phase involves gathering information about the prospects' needs, desires and goals. The gathering process will vary depending upon the product or service you offer. Regardless, it is important that you express sincere interest in your prospects' objectives, not yours. Prospects must feel that you are attentive to their needs.

During this phase it is often possible (without mentioning any specific names) to relate their needs with those of other clients whom you serve. It is often appropriate to draw a parallel between your prospects and the clients who referred you. You can do this as long as you do not divulge any information which your existing clients may feel should not be shared. I often ask my clients if they mind if I let their friends know that I have set up an IRA to help them retire comfortably or a college plan for their kids. As long as they do not object, I will make the appropriate analogies without being overly specific. Once again, this process helps your prospects get used to the fact that you work strictly on referrals. When you feel that you have a complete understanding of your prospects' needs, desires or goals, begin the third phase of the appointment.

The third phase involves presenting your prospects with the products or services that you feel will best help them meet their objectives. Oftentimes the best product for them may not be the most profitable one for you. Some salespeople, who have not yet unlocked the secret to getting referrals, will recommend a product with the highest profit margin or commission. After all, once the product is sold, the relationship with the client, for most salespeople, has ended.

For a sales professional who works through referrals, this is certainly not the case. Hundreds of times I have sold products that had much lower commissions than other products I could have sold. I could have easily convinced hundreds of my clients to invest in products that would have made me more money but would have been less appropriate in achieving their goals. I could never do this. The Referral Cycle with these clients would immediately come to an end. Compromising my integrity might be profitable in the short term, but it would surely erode the relationship that I worked so hard to develop.

I do not make as much money per sale as many of my competitors do, but never in my life will I worry from where my next prospect will come. My prospect pool is overflowing with referrals. I have had to hire additional associates and share my prospects with them. At one point, my prospect pool had over eight hundred referrals for me to contact.

The three keys to successful referral generation are: integrity, informing your clients what they should expect of you, and telling your clients what you expect of them ... specifically, referrals.

Everyone has heard the expression "Live by the sword, die by the sword." It is also true that a salesperson can "Live by the referral, die by the referral." If you work solely on referrals and inflict an injustice on a client, the word will spread to your other clients like wildfire. (Of course, I have no personal experience to support this, although the thought scares me!) When you begin working strictly on referrals, both the quality and the quantity of your sales will improve.

Once clients have agreed to do business with you and it is time to take the order, you should interrupt the paperwork, look your clients in the eyes, and say the following:

> *"Oh! This is something very important.* (Pass a legal pad and pen across the table to your clients.) *You know that I work strictly by referrals. Would you be kind enough to write down the names of a few folks who might benefit from my services? You don't need to worry about how much money they make or if you think they may already have satisfied their goals. What I'll do is give them a call and treat them the same way I treated you. I'll explain to them that it is not important to*

> *me that we do business. All that matters is that if they appreciate the time we share together, if they respect my integrity, and if they feel that they learned something during our meeting, that they will be willing to pass my name on to someone else who may benefit from my services. I really appreciate this. I depend on good clients, like you, to keep my business rolling."*

This is crucial! Look at what this approach does. You are telling your clients that you will treat their referrals with the same respect you afforded them. You are reminding them of the agreement they made when they first set up this meeting with you. You are telling them that you will tell their referrals that you will not push for business. You are complimenting them by telling them that they are good clients. And most important, in the middle of taking the order or writing an application, you have paused to express the importance of getting referrals. They know where you make your money. They also know that you do not make it until the paperwork is signed. For you to interrupt this process and ask them for some names displays tremendous confidence and will most likely not encounter an objection. In Chapter Thirteen, you will learn how the referral process evolves to the point where you don't even ask for a list of names. But in the beginning when you first establish your referral generation program, this step is mandatory.

Admiral Nimitz once said to a junior officer, "When in command, command." During the Appointment phase you are in full command of your prospect. This is your ideal opportunity for a referral sale which parallels your product sale. Your request for referrals will be fulfilled. Your clients already know that it is in their best interest to purchase your product. They also know it is in their best interest to provide you with referrals. Take charge!

If your prospects decide not to do business with you, it does not mean that the Referral Cycle has ended. After all, they may need time to think about your recommendations or to discuss them with a trusted friend, relative, or business associate. This should not stop you from asking for referrals. Remember, they had previously agreed to meet with you on the condition that they would be willing to give you referrals as long as they respected your integrity, and felt that they benefitted in some way from the time you spent together. Remind them of this and you will rarely encounter an objection. If you do encounter an objection, it may very well help you identify the reason why the prospects have not yet been converted into clients.

You must use common sense in determining how hard to push for names at this time. You should always ask, remind them of their agreement, and listen carefully to their response. Often you will have the pleasant task of contacting them several weeks later thanking them for the referrals who have become clients and reminding them that you should meet again soon. They will most likely agree. After all, if their friends, relatives, or business associates became clients, maybe they need to give your product a second look.

I cannot over-emphasize the fact that presenting a parallel referral sale along with the product sale greatly enhances the odds of your doing business with your prospects. Too many salespeople fear that pushing for referrals could jeopardize the sale of their product or service. Pushing for referrals alone will, but asking for them after an effective referral presentation process has been utilized will only serve to enhance your odds of bringing home a paycheck now and in the future. When you know that you have a stack of referrals in the top left hand drawer of your desk, it takes great pressure off of the sales presentation. Most salespeople starve for prospects; therefore, they have to sell their product on every appointment because they do not know when their next selling opportunity will come. This causes them to subconsciously be more aggressive on the appointment which hurts their chances of making a sale and getting referrals.

The point is that getting referrals provides you with a comfort zone and allows you to operate under much less strenuous conditions. You feel more comfortable with your product, your prospect and yourself. Your prospects sense this calm confidence; it helps them to feel more at ease with you.

The parallel sale feeds on itself and allows you to become more profitable with less stress. It frees up what used to be your prospecting time so that you may use this time to provide your clients with additional services. Once again, these additional personal services will enhance your argument for getting even more referrals, and this wonderful cycle continues, and continues and continues.

Chapter Ten

Product Delivery

Very often the Product Delivery phase provides salespeople with the last opportunity for face-to-face contact with their clients. All salespeople know that they can have the most influence on a prospect or client during a personal visit. In Chapter Four we discussed the evolution of the sales process during the past century. As you may recall, over the past forty years salespeople have depended less and less on quality personal contact. The Product Delivery phase provides you with another occasion to have a positive impact on your clients. This frequently takes place shortly after the completion of the Appointment phase. The significance of the timeliness of your visit is that the clients' previous positive experience with you is still fresh in their minds. You have worked hard to develop this trusting relationship and should nuture it at this time.

Almost every selling profession has some type of Product Delivery phase. The delivery phase is more

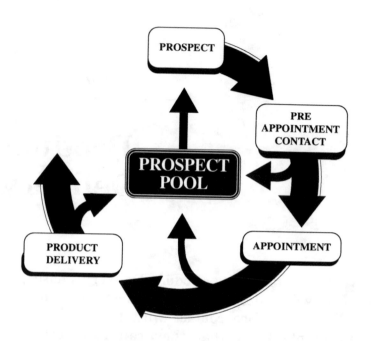

obvious with some products and services than others. For example, in the life insurance industry it involves the agent physically handing the policy to the client. In real estate, it would be the day the customer goes to closing on the home or property. For a computer programmer, it would be the day that the system is installed and useable. In advertising, it would be the day that the ad runs in the publication. Whatever your profession, you should identify the precise moment that your product or service becomes of value to your customer, and at this point the Product Delivery phase begins.

Besides the physical delivery of the product or service, you should strive to accomplish two objectives. You must reinforce both your commitment to your clients and your clients' commitment to you. The goal is to strengthen the two-way relationship which has already begun to develop. Here is an example of what you can say to help reinforce your commitment to your clients.

> *"I want you to know that I value your trust in me and I look forward to providing you with the best service possible. If you ever have any questions or need any advice on how to make the best use of your purchase, please call me. Here is my home telephone number. If it happens to be after hours, please don't hesitate to call me there. It is important to me that you know I stand behind my product one hundred percent and I will do anything in my power to keep you a satisified client."*

By reinforcing your commitment to your clients you are assuring them that you will be caring for their well-being and peace of mind. It is important to review the benefits of the product or service purchased and to make certain that your clients fully understand how to make the most effective use of their purchase. By the time this meeting is over there should be no doubt in the clients' mind as to your dedication toward their well-being. Only after this is accomplished will your clients be ready to entrust you with others for whom they care.

Here is another powerful script to help you reinforce your clients' commitment to you.

"I'm sure by now you realize that I work strictly through referrals. I am constantly striving to bring my clients even greater service by improving my business. I have a very important question for you and would appreciate your giving this some thought. Is there any one thing that you would like to see me change or improve upon which would increase the likelihood of my getting referrals from you in the future?"

This script, if relayed with sincerity (there's no reason it shouldn't be), will greatly enhance your opportunities for getting referrals. Your clients will respect your honesty and will either share a recommendation with you or feel obligated to pass your name on to others who they feel would benefit from dealing with a salesperson of such integrity.

During the Product Delivery phase you also have an opportunity to show your appreciation for referrals that have already been provided to you. It is important to give your clients a status report on the names they gave you. This helps to reaffirm their confidence in knowing that you have done well with the referrals they have given you and may inspire them to give you more.

Oftentimes, clients will hold back in the beginning, giving you only a few names to see how you do with them. This "referral status report" will usually prompt your clients to give you more referrals. You can also use this time to gather expanded information on referrals that you have previously received but have not yet contacted. Most important, you have the opportunity to once again ask for referrals if you have not yet received any.

The following is an example of what you may say during product delivery.

> "I appreciate the opportunity of doing business with you. I know that you are very happy with the service I have provided you and I promise to be here should you have any questions or need further help in the future. I'd like to thank you for sharing your friends, Ray and Dorothy, with me. I met with them last week and I'm sure they told you that they were very happy with the time we shared together. It really means a lot to me that you trust me enough to share the names of some of your friends and business associates with me. As I promised you in the past, I will never say anything or treat the referrals you give me in a way that would cause a bad reflection on you. Obviously, you would never provide me with another referral. I look forward to a longlasting relationship with both you and with anyone else I meet. Which reminds me, I haven't had a chance to meet the Johnsons yet. Could you tell me when might be the best time to contact them?"

Later during the Product Delivery phase you should ask your clients what kind of reactions they have received from others with whom they have discussed you, your product or your service. A simple question will usually provide you with a lot of information.

In Chapter Thirteen, we will discuss the Evolution of the Referral Process. In Level Two of the referral process you will learn that it is the clients' responsibility to speak with the referrals they gave you to determine if they have an interest. If your clients have not yet contacted you concerning any responses they may have had, the Product Delivery phase provides you with an excellent opportunity to discuss with them any interest their friends or colleagues may have expressed.

The following is an example of what you could say during the Product Delivery phase when you are in Level Two of the referral process.

> *"Have you had a chance to hand out any of my brochures to your friends or have you talked with anyone about the services I have to offer? ... What was their reaction?"*

You must listen carefully to your clients' responses and study their expressions as you ask these questions. This will help you determine if, indeed, your clients have been effective in spreading the good word of the value you have to share with the community. You will often find that your clients want to be a greater help to you but may still feel uncomfortable in knowing exactly how to approach their friends or acquaintances. This question provides you with a tremendous opportunity to further educate your valuable clients in the ways they can help you grow your business.

By the time this phase is over your clients should feel grateful that they have chosen to do business with you. They should not feel that they have helped you by purchasing your product or service; rather, they should be proud that they helped you by providing you with referrals.

You have been able to help your clients by providing a product which fills a specific need, desire or goal. Your clients have helped you by providing you with referrals so that your business will continue to grow. This two way relationship can flourish for many years with both the clients and salespeople receiving tremendous benefits. In the next chapter, we will discuss the different types of service that must be extended in order to maintain a high level of trust.

Chapter Eleven

Service and Follow-Up

Service is the performance of any helpful or professional work or activity for a person, family, organization or business. The Service and Follow-Up phase of the Referral Cycle provides you with ongoing opportunities to maintain contact with your clients. Anytime that you have contact with your clients you encounter the possibility of getting more referrals. The quality and quantity of service will help enhance the quality and quantity of the referrals you receive. High quality service helps to create a very professional and caring image which clients are not afraid of sharing with their friends, family and business associates; a high quantity of service helps keep you and your product fresh in the minds of your clients.

For many salespeople, the Product Delivery phase represents the end of the relationship with their clients. There are three reasons why this happens. First, the nature of the business may not require any additional service. Second, although there may be a

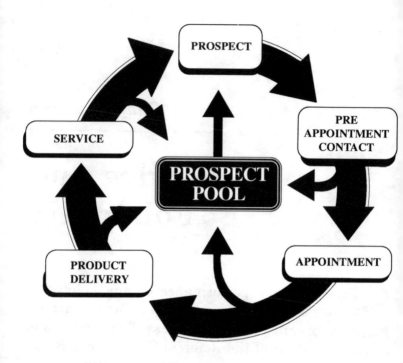

need for continued service, salespeople are so pre-occupied with prospecting or selling that they cannot devote adequate time toward providing adequate service. Third, salespeople may not realize that providing their clients with quality service can benefit them in expanding the quality and quantity of their business. What it comes down to is **no need, no time,** or **no benefit**. In the following paragraphs we will discuss each of these reasons in greater detail.

No Need - It is tough to be of service to clients who do not expect or require additional service. Creativity is the key to creating the need for value added service. The best service is that which is provided to clients when they least expect it. Salespeople providing value added service can make a difference by separating themselves from their competitors. A simple thank-you note, a birthday card, or a six-month follow-up will do wonders to keep your name fresh in your clients' minds.

No Time - Many salespeople give inadequate service because they believe that they do not have time to devote to the task. In any sales profession, money is made by having contact with prospects and selling a product. Most salespeople would agree that a large majority of their time is spent prospecting. There are only so many hours in a day. Many salespeople believe that providing adequate service would take too much away from their prospecting time. Once again, we are faced with the "Which came first, the chicken or the egg?" scenario. It must be understood that if sufficient time is given to service, the referral business will grow and less time will have to be spent on prospecting. In fact, when done properly, servicing **is** prospecting. To effectively utilize the opportunities created by the Service phase of the Referral Cycle, time must be set aside and dedicated to its purpose.

No Benefit - The greatest benefit in providing quality service is, once again, the referrals that it generates. There is no more powerful tool in marketing a product than happy clients.

Maintaining longlasting relationships with your clients through frequent and helpful service enhances your reputation, the reputation of your product, and the likelihood of your name being passed on to friends, family, and business associates who have not been exposed to such quality service in the past. Of course, as previously discussed, another benefit is the additional time you save on prospecting because of the referrals that will soon be coming your way.

The type of service which is appropriate to the product varies from industry to industry. Some follow-up services, however, should be extended regardless of your profession.

Thank-You Cards - Professionally printed thank-you cards which extend your appreciation and are personally signed are very effective and always create an impression upon your clients. The cards should have slots that allow you to insert your business card. It is very important that you ask your clients to pass your business card to someone else who they feel may benefit from your services.

Birthday Cards - If you can tactfully obtain birth date information, birthday cards should be sent to all members of the family or business who have benefitted from your product or service. It is often appropriate to write a short personalized message in the card. The envelope should be handwritten and the card signed in ink. Never use computerized labels on a birthday card.

Annual Follow-Ups - Once a year, on or about the anniversary of the initial sale, your clients should be personally contacted. The purpose of this contact is to both reassure your clients that you are still interested in their well-being and to determine if their needs, desires or goals have changed over the past year. If your clients are satisfied with you, it is a very appropriate time to once again request the names of friends, family and business associates who may benefit from you or your product.

Below is an example of what I say during a typical annual follow-up:

> *"Hello, Ray. This is Scott Kramnick, how are you? ... As I promised when we first did business, this is my 'official' once-a-year call to let you know that I haven't forgotten about you. You should have received your annual report by now. Do you have any questions? ...I also want to make sure you and Dorothy have received your birthday cards and quarterly newsletters. What do you think of my newsletter? ...Terrific. I'll let you go now, don't forget, you've got my number if you need any help. Please keep me in mind when talking to your friends and business associates. As you know, Ray, I depend on quality clients like you and Dorothy to keep me in business. I look forward to seeing you soon. Goodbye."*

The following services may be more appropriate in some industries than others. Once again, creativity in service should be the focus.

Quarterly Newsletters - Quarterly newsletters are an effective way of maintaining contact with your clients on a regular basis. It is very important that the newsletter be designed to be informative. It can discuss additional uses for the products which have been sold, or help educate the client in the industry which you represent. Its purpose should not be to sell a particular product. If your clients perceive this newsletter as a pitch for more sales, it will soon be regarded as junk mail and will not be read.

Personal Notes - It is very effective to send a personal note or card to your clients expressing your appreciation for their trust in you and your product. This need only be done once every year or two. The note should always express thanks for any referrals you have received. Following is an example of what I hand write in my notes to clients.

> *Dear Joe,*
> *Just a quick note to let you know it's been an honor over the past year to have the opportunity to play a small part in helping you achieve your goals. Thanks for referring Ray and Dorothy to me. I promise to provide them with the same quality service*

I have extended to you. I look forward to seeing you soon.

Best Wishes,
Scott

Product Updates - When appropriate, inform your clients of recent updates or changes to the products they purchased from you. Take care not to appear to degrade the product they originally purchased. The purpose of the update should be to keep the client abreast of product trends. In financial planning this may involve a discussion of changing interest rate trends or the conversion of term insurance to permanent insurance. Real estate agents who inform their clients of home improvement ideas such as the value of waterproofing their deck or sealing their driveway will separate themselves from their competition. They are creating a reason to have additional contact with their clients while extending advice that will most likely add to the resale value of their clients' homes. The average family lives in their home for approximately seven years. I would be willing to bet that most do not remember the name of the real estate agent who originally sold them their home.

Client Questionnaires - Oftentimes, it is very useful to periodically send your clients a questionnaire. The purpose of the questionnaire is to update your records and refamiliarize your clients with all of the products or services you offer. It also helps keep you in the forefront of their memory and gives your clients an opportunity to provide you with more referrals. At the end of this chapter is a copy of the letter I send to each of my clients along with the attached client questionnaire. You can easily adapt the letter and the questionnaire to suit your particular business.

The services previously listed are a few ideas that you should consider adapting to your business. You can most certainly come up with other services specific to your industry that will help reinforce a positive image of you in the minds of your clients.

When you establish the specific methods you will utilize to help you maintain closer contact with your clients and build stronger relationships, you must consider the system you will use to keep track of important information and dates. This system can be a simple tickler file made up of index cards very similar to that discussed in Chapter Fourteen, or you may decide to purchase one of the many computer software programs available on the market. Whatever system you decide upon, the low cost and short time to establish and maintain such a system will pay for itself many times over.

It goes without saying that any problems your clients may encounter should be corrected swiftly, accurately and courteously. The mishandling of client complaints will put an immediate end to any hopes of getting future referrals. The satisfactory correction of any difficulties clients encounter actually improves their opinion of your ability to deal with their needs. Oftentimes, when handled correctly, these negatives can be turned into positives.

This chapter on the Service phase completes our discussion of the Referral Cycle. Keep in mind that all phases are operating simultaneously and no one phase can be ignored. When properly executed, the Referral Cycle operates like a well-oiled piece of machinery and will pay dividends for life. In the next chapter, we will expand upon the ways that you may enhance both the number and usefulness of referrals provided to you through the effective use of the Referral Cycle.

On the following pages you will find a sample letter and questionnaire which you can adapt to your particular business situation.

Date

Name
Address
City, State Zip

Dear _____,

We at Kramnick & Associates are honored to have had the opportunity to be of service to you during the past year. In our continuing efforts to provide you with the best possible service, we ask that you take a moment to complete the following Kramnick & Associates Client Questionnaire.

This Questionnaire serves to update our records and gives you an opportunity to request any additional information or services that you may require. We hope that you find this Questionnaire, along with our quarterly newsletter, a benefit worthy of your time.

Should you have any family members or friends who might appreciate us and the services we provide, please note their names on the bottom of the Questionnaire. We wish you and your family a healthy and prosperous coming year and we hope to see you in the near future.

Sincerely,

Scott A. Kramnick

SAK/pjk
Enc.

KRAMNICK & ASSOCIATES CLIENT QUESTIONNAIRE

NAME: _____   DATE: _____

SECTION 1: Since our last discussion I have:

_____ changed jobs   _____ been promoted
_____ married   _____ retired
_____ started a business   _____ won the lottery

A family member has:

_____ been accepted to college _____ married
_____ graduated   _____ received an award
                                           or scholarship

SECTION 2: We expect/had a child in _____(month)
We expect/had a grandchild in _____ (month)
We adopted a child in _____ (month)
Name(s) _____ Birthday(s) _____
Name(s) _____ Birthday(s) _____

SECTION 3: I am interested in or would like more information about:

_____ Ways to reduce taxes   _____ Mutual Funds
_____ Improving my IRA   _____ Retirement Planning
_____ Alternatives to CD's   _____ Mortgage Acceleration
_____ Disability Income   _____ Estate Planning
_____ Converting term ins.   _____ Life Insurance
_____ Employee Benefit Plans   _____ Mortgage Protection
_____ Group Insurance   _____ Business Insurance
_____ Maximizing Pension   _____ Long-Term Care

Please let us know if we can be of service to any of your friends, family or co-workers ...

Name_____   Name_____
Phone_____   Phone_____
Best time to contact _____   Best time to contact _____
Comments: Comments:

PART III

BUILDING ON SUCCESS

Decisive people make progress toward their goals when they are right and make progress in their lives when they are wrong.

- Scott Kramnick

Chapter Twelve

Referral Enhancement

In referral enhancement you must be concerned with two areas - quality and quantity. As you become more experienced in making effective use of the Referral Cycle, both of these areas will automatically improve. In this chapter we will outline some basic principles of which you should constantly be aware in order to take advantage of every opportunity you encounter. First, we will discuss enhancing the quantity of the referrals you will receive.

The easiest way to increase the number of the referrals you receive is to make sure that you get referrals from every one of your clients. We have already discussed the Referral Cycle and the activities in which you should engage to improve your chances of getting referrals. Getting referrals from every client is a matter of attention to detail. If you are not getting referrals from all of your clients, you should review the contacts you had with your clients and find out which phase or phases of the parallel referral sale require improvement. A simple way to determine this is to ask your clients why they feel uncomfortable giving you referrals. Once you are told, it will be easy to retrace your steps along the Referral Cycle and make the appropriate adjustments. In the future, you will not repeat the mistake.

> *"Ray, as you know, I work strictly through referrals and depend on quality clients like yourself to help me grow my business. I sense that you feel uncomfortable providing me with names of people you know. I'm convinced that you believe in my product and service. Have I done something to lose your trust?"*

If you have provided your clients with outstanding service, if the product they purchased fulfilled their needs, and if you have been effective in building a good relationship, then this is a very fair question to ask. Your clients will respect the honesty and integrity of your question. Without fail, you will learn something from this contact which will help you make future adjustments that will alleviate the problem. Your growth in experience will lead to more referrals.

Another very effective way of getting greater numbers of referrals begins by understanding the feelings of your clients. Near the end of your appointments, at the time you make the request for names, your clients may very well be approaching "burnout." Knowing this, it would **not** be wise to ask them for the name, address, telephone number, marital status, age, and occupation of a referral, along with any other pertinent information which would certainly be of use to you. They may provide you with this information for the first referral they give you, and may be kind enough to extend themselves into providing this for the second referral; however, they will soon catch on and may hesitate to give you five or ten more names.

The best approach to use is what I call the "Deli Method." Think of the last time you went to your local delicatessen. You stood in front of the counter and, with a smile from the deli employee, were greeted with, "May I help you?" You then said, "Sure, I'd like a pound of smoked ham, please." As the deli employee wrapped your order you were then asked a brilliant question, **"And what else?"** You then said, "How about a half of a pound of Swiss cheese." While your cheese was being wrapped, another question surfaced from your cheerful deli employee, **"And what else?"** These questions were flying at you pretty quickly, so you responded, "Give me a pound of that potato salad, please." You will not believe this but once again one of the greatest salespeople in history came back with another line. You guessed it ... **"And what else?"**

Okay, what is my point? You should use this deli method in asking for referrals. It works likes this:

> **Salesperson:** *"Ray, I know you appreciate the time that I have spent with you this afternoon. Would you mind giving me the name of someone who might also appreciate the same integrity that I have extended to you? Just a first name would be fine."*

Ray: *"Well, you might want to talk to Tim."*

Salesperson: *"And who else?"*

Ray: *"Well, I work with a guy named Jack."*

Salesperson: *"And who else?"*

Ray: *"My brother, Steve."*

Salesperson: *"And who else?"*

The deli method of extracting referrals provides phenomenal results. I have received up to forty or fifty names from one client using this method. It is not important to get the remainder of the information right away. Remember that in Chapter Nine we said that you should ask for referrals before the paperwork is completed. Oftentimes, you will be meeting with both a husband and a wife, or two or more business associates. Once you have received a list of first names (which you have listed double spaced on a legal pad) you can pass the legal pad to one of the spouses or other business associates while you complete the paperwork with the other. Simply ask them if they wouldn't mind adding the last name, telephone number and any other information they feel might be useful. Getting the names is the key. If there is no time to fill in the rest of the information, this can be accomplished during the Product Delivery phase or at a later date.

Another way to increase the quantity of referrals you receive is to make sure that you try to get referrals at each phase of the Referral Cycle. Once clients give you referrals, you should not assume they have no one left to refer to you. People who have been in sales for more than a couple of years know that their best source for new sales is often their existing clients. Likewise, the best source for referrals is your existing clients. Anytime you have contact with your clients, you should determine if they are pleased with your service. If they respond favorably, you should always ask if they know someone else who could benefit from you, your product, or your service.

> *"Hi, Ray... I'm glad to hear you're happy with the business we've done together. Ray, by now you certainly know that I work strictly by referrals. Would you happen to know anyone else you feel may benefit from the value I've extended to you? It would mean a lot to me if you could share the names of a couple of folks whom I promise to treat with the utmost respect. How about one of the companies you do business with? Is there anyone there who you feel can benefit from the services I offer?"*

We will now discuss ways that you can enhance the quality of the referrals you receive. You will soon read in Chapter Thirteen that your referral quality will automatically improve as your referral gathering techniques evolve. There are some things, however, that you should begin paying attention to immediately.

The easiest and most obvious task is to get as much information as possible about your referrals before you contact them. This can be done by asking your clients specific questions about the individuals they have referred. While being careful not to appear to be too intrusive, you can obtain key bits of information which will help you during your initial contact with your prospects.

> *"Ray, I thank you for giving me Joe's name. Would you mind telling me if he is married or has any children? ...Is it best to contact Joe at home or do you think he may prefer I call him at work? ...What type of work does he do? ...How did you folks meet? ...Which of the services I offer do you feel he would find of greatest value?"*

If you have established the parallel referral sale and have taken advantage of each phase of the Referral Cycle you will find your clients more than willing to provide you with this type of information. Be sincere and you will be trusted.

A big mistake many salespeople make is in not asking for referrals from someone who they feel has a low income or may not be very influential within the community. Some of my greatest leads have come from clients with whom I have done the least amount of business. Remember, almost everyone has a mother, father, or works with or for someone who makes more money than they do. Society is not accustomed to salespeople who sincerely take good care of people with little wealth. It is common sense that if the wealthy realize what great care you take of their children or their employees, they will also realize that you will most certainly take great care of them. After all, they know that you stand to make more money from them than you made from those who referred them to you. The greater care you take of your smallest clients, the greater trust your potentially larger clients will have in you. No one likes to do business with salespeople who appear to be chasing after the big dollars while stepping on everyone else along their way.

> *"Ray, would you happen to know anyone who may benefit from my services? It's important that you don't try to qualify them by how much money they make. You know that I work strictly through referrals and I must tell you that some of my largest client accounts have come from the parents, friends or bosses of my clients with small accounts. Whom might you know who could benefit from my service?"*

While reading this, you may feel it is hypocritical to pay so much attention to the little guys just so that you can meet the big guys. On the contrary, in this case everybody wins. Once again, I must repeat, it makes good business sense to provide the best possible service to anyone and everyone you encounter.

Finally, the greatest way to enhance the quality of your referrals is to put your clients to work for you. Do not be afraid to ask your clients for the names of their parents or employers. Your clients will most likely have a much closer relationship with their relatives, friends or business associates than you may ever hope to have. They know what excites their friends; and they know what turns them off. Clients who truly believe in you will do wonders when it comes to convincing someone they know to consider you, your product, or your service.

Your clients will open doors for you that you never dreamed possible. They will walk you into homes, they will set up appointments for you with their employers, and they will introduce you to some of the most influential people they know. All you have to do is demonstrate your integrity and treat them with respect, sincerity, and loyalty. These actions, in conjunction with the activities associated with the Referral Cycle, will eventually bring your prospecting days to an end. You will no longer have to prospect. Your clients will do it for you. We call this the Evolution of the Referral Process and we will discuss it in the next chapter.

Chapter Thirteen

Evolution of the Referral Process

The ultimate goal of the referral generation system is to bring your prospecting days to an end. You do this by getting your clients to do the prospecting for you. It takes time, however, to teach your clients how to work for you. You cannot afford to sit idly while waiting for your clients to bring you prospects. This would certainly lead to disaster. In this chapter you will learn how the referral process evolves through five levels, eventually ending up at our final goal.

Level One. Your first task is to fill up your prospect pool so that you can put an end to cold calls, mass mailings, and expensive advertising. This task is simple. Using the information contained in this book, you talk about referrals during each phase of the Referral Cycle. At the appropriate time, when you are convinced that your clients have warmed up to the idea of giving you referrals, you say the following:

> *"Oh! This is something very important.*
> (You pass a legal pad and pen across the
> table to your clients.) *You know that I*
> *work strictly by referrals. Would you be*
> *kind enough to write down the names of*
> *a few folks who might benefit from my*
> *services? You don't need to worry about*
> *how much money they make or if you*
> *think they may already have satisfied*
> *their goals. What I'll do is give them a call*
> *and treat them the same way I treated you.*
> *I'll explain to them that it is not important*
> *to me that we do business. I'll tell them all*
> *that matters is if they appreciate the time*
> *we share together, if they respect my*
> *integrity, and, if they feel they learned*
> *something during our meeting, they will*
> *be willing to pass my name on to someone*
> *else who may benefit from my services. I*
> *really appreciate this. I depend on good*
> *clients, like you, to keep my business*
> *rolling."*

Once again, these words can be slightly adapted to
suit your particular business.

You remain at Level One until you have gathered
enough names to satisfy your prospecting needs for
the foreseeable future. Generally, this can be accomplished during a dozen or so appointments and
should yield approximately one hundred names. You
now have a significant number of leads with which
to work and are ready to step up to Level Two.

Level Two. You gather a list of names just as you did in Level One. The difference is that at the time your clients give you the list, you ask your clients to mention to the referrals that they were very pleased with your product or service and that you will be giving them a call to share some ideas. Within two weeks, you call your clients back and ask if anyone they spoke with expressed interest in meeting with you. From this point on, the interested referrals would become your main focus.

> *"You know that I work strictly by referrals.* (You pass them them a legal pad. As they begin to write the names of people they know, you continue speaking.) *Would you be kind enough to write down the names of a few folks who might benefit from my services? You don't need to worry about how much money they make or if you think they may already have satisfied their goals.* **It would mean a lot to me if over the next week you would mention to these folks that you were very pleased with my services and that it may be in their best interest to set up a time to meet with me. In about a week I'll give you a call and you can let me know which of these folks seem the most interested.** *I promise you that I will treat each of your referrals with the same respect and integrity that I have extended to you. I'll explain to them that it is not important to me that we do business. I'll tell them all that matters is if they appreciate the time we*

> *share together, if they respect my integrity, and if they feel they learned something during our meeting, they will be willing to pass my name on to someone else who may benefit from my services. I really appreciate this. I depend on good clients, like you, to keep my business rolling."*

Level Three. With your prospect pool full and your clients actively supporting your business, you no longer require long lists of names to contact. At this point, you ask your clients to inform family members, friends, or business associates of your product or service. You tell your clients that you are not going to burden them by asking for long lists of names, but that you would appreciate it if they would make a mental note of anyone who seems interested. You will find it helpful to provide your clients with brochures which outline all the products and services you offer. Ask your clients to give these brochures to their acquaintances and to encourage each of them to take the time to read through the brochure. You then let them know that you will call them in a week to get the names of those who expressed an interest.

The only difference between Level Two and Level Three is that the names you end up with in Level Three have all indicated their desire to meet with you. If you have properly graduated from one level to the other you will soon find that the names continue to pile up and, more important, your newer clients have become accustomed to their friends talking about you, your product or your service.

Although they do not realize it, their friends have prepared them for the work they will soon be doing for you.

"You know that I work strictly by referrals. I would be honored if you would do me a favor and give some of your friends, family and business associates one of my brochures. (You pass them several brochures.) *It would be really helpful to me if you would take a moment to explain to them how much you value my service and that you feel they may benefit from meeting with me. Please make a mental note of anyone who seemed interested. I will not burden you by asking you for a list of names, but if you would be kind enough to allow me to give you a call next week and get the names of those interested individuals, I would greatly appreciate it. I promise you I will treat any referrals you give me with the same respect and dignity that I have treated you. I'll explain to them that it is not important to me that we do business. I'll tell them all that matters is if they appreciate the time we share together, if they respect my integrity, and if they feel they learned something during our meeting, they will be willing to pass my name on to someone else who may benefit from my services. I really appreciate this. I depend on good clients, like you, to keep my business rolling."*

Level Four. By this time your confidence in what your clients will do for you is overwhelming. More and more of your prospecting work is being passed on to those who believe in you. You no longer ask for names. At this level you ask your clients to talk to some people about you and to give you a call if they run into someone who expresses interest. While at this level, it is important to remember that during every phase of the Referral Cycle you remind your clients of their responsibility to call you if they know someone to whom you may be of service. Once your client base grows, you will have dozens, and soon hundreds, of clients talking to people about you, your product or service. You will never totally leave the fourth level, but you will soon add Level Five to your process.

> *"You know that I work strictly by referrals. I would be honored if you would do me a favor and give some of your friends, family and business associates one of my brochures.* (You pass them several brochures.) *It would be really helpful to me if you would take a moment to explain to them how much you value my service and that you feel they may benefit from meeting with me. Please make a mental note of anyone who seemed interested. I will not burden you by asking you for a list of names, but if you would be kind enough to call me with the names of anyone who seemed interested I would greatly appreciate it. I promise you I will*

treat any referrals you give me with the same respect and dignity that I have treated you. I'll explain to them that it is not important to me that we do business. I'll tell them all that matters is if they appreciate the time we share together, if they respect my integrity, and if they feel they learned something during our meeting, they will be willing to pass my name on to someone else who may benefit from my services. I really appreciate this. I depend on good clients, like you, to keep my business rolling."

Level Five. By the time you get to Level Five, your clients have grown accustomed to working for you. Their trust in you has grown to heights few salespeople ever come to appreciate. At this level you ask your clients to give your telephone number to interested friends, family members and business associates. You then coach your clients on the types of things to say which would heighten the interest of the people with whom they come in contact. It is at this level that your prospecting days come to an end. Your efforts are concentrated only on teaching your existing clients what to say and what not to say to the people who they feel are most able to benefit from you, your product or your service. You also tell your clients to explain to their friends, family members and business associates that you work only on referrals and that because of this, they do not have to worry about being pushed, hounded, or harassed.

You know that I work strictly by referrals. I would be honored if you would do me a favor and give some of your friends, family and business associates one of my brochures. (You pass them several brochures.) *It would be really helpful to me if you would take a moment to explain to them how much you value my service and that you feel they may benefit from meeting with me. I will not burden you by asking for a list of names. But I would ask, once again, that you encourage your friends, family members, and business associates to call me. I promise you I will treat any referrals you give me with the same respect and dignity that I have treated you. I'll explain to them that it is not important to me that we do business. I'll tell them all that matters is if they appreciate the time we share together, if they respect my integrity, and if they feel they learned something during our meeting, they will be willing to pass my name on to someone else who may benefit from my services. I really appreciate this. I depend on good clients, like you, to keep my business rolling."*

Level Five calls on you to make an effort to teach your clients what to say and what not to say when talking to their friends, relatives and business associates about you, your product and your service. For example, if you are a financial planner who has just sold your clients life insurance policies, you would want to make sure that when they mention you to other prospects they also mention that you offer mutual funds, CD's, disability insurance, etc. The reason for this is that foremost in your clients' minds is the fact that they purchased life insurance from you and without the proper instruction they may describe you as only a life insurance salesperson. Not that there is anything wrong with life insurance salespeople, but some prospects your clients speak with may already have life insurance and therefore will have no interest in seeking further information. This is why it is critical for you to teach your clients how to describe you, your products and your services.

If you are a real estate agent who helps families find and purchase their homes, it is important that your clients and their acquaintances are aware that you also help clients locate and purchase investment property, farm land and office space.

As a computer systems consultant who just sold a business a new computer network, you would want the business owner and users to know that you also offer personal computers, software and programming instruction. If they are telling others that they purchased hardware from you and make no mention of the broad range of your capabilities, it is very likely that prospects who are happy with their current hardware would have no interest in meeting with you. When your clients are taught to make mention of your diverse capabilities, they will open doors for you that may otherwise be left locked.

After studying the five levels of the Evolution of the Referral Process you may wonder why we do not begin with Level Three or Level Four. The answer is twofold. First, it is important that you become confident in the fact that your clients are willing to give you referrals. The quickest way to gain this confidence is to leave an appointment with a long list of names. If you are not having success in getting these names, then it means that somewhere the Referral Cycle is breaking down. You must identify where the breakdown has occurred and correct it. When you begin receiving referrals from the vast majority of your clients, then you know the system works and you are ready to graduate to the next level. If you had begun with Level Three or Level Four it would take a lot longer for you to identify your strengths and weaknesses. The first two levels are your training ground.

The second reason you must evolve through the process is because your clients need to become comfortable with working for you. As you progress through the five levels, your clients have been referred to you through other clients, and they through others, and they through others and they through others. Your clients have accepted that you work strictly on referrals and are willing to do their part, just as their friends, relatives, and business associates are doing. The evolution of the referral process is complete.

Chapter Fourteen

Tracking Referrals

If you have been in sales for any length of time, you have most likely developed a method by which you keep track of your prospects. Some salespeople track their leads by writing them in their appointment book. Others keep some type of a "tickler file." Still others haphazardly accumulate business cards, telephone messages, scrap sheets of paper or names on cocktail napkins. Of course, different systems work for different people.

Some salespeople and businesses find great value in making use of one of the many client or prospect management computer programs currently available. Many of them are advertised in software or selling publications. For your convenience, I have included at the end of this chapter the names and telephone numbers of some of these companies. I would encourage you to compare these products carefully before making an investment.

The system outlined in this chapter is archaic compared to the software currently available but it has worked well for me and I still use it today. If you have a prospect tracking system that you feel could be improved upon, or if you have not yet developed an effective workable system, this chapter will be of use to you.

To either lose a name or not follow through in contacting a prospect would certainly not be considered effective prospect management. The following system, when adhered to, will guarantee that you never let a prospect fall through the cracks. It is a simple "tickler file" set up with index cards.

As soon as you return from an appointment you should transfer all of the information regarding any referrals you receive onto index cards. If you are in your office and a client calls you with a referral, you should immediately enter the information in the proper format on an index card. A sample of the index card along with a brief description of each entry follows.

NAME ①	② TELEPHONE NUMBER
	DATE
⑤	⑥
REFERRING PERSON ③ RELATIONSHIP ④	

1. Enter the name of the referral/prospect.

2. Enter the telephone number of the referral.

3. Enter the name of the referring person.

4. Enter the relationship between the referring person and the referral. This may be something as simple as "brother," "best friend," or "boss."

5. Enter any information you are given that might be useful when you have contact with the referral. This may be information you receive from the referring person. It could also be information you obtain during telephone contact with the referral. Any bit of information you obtain should be written in this area for future reference.

6. Enter the date on which you are required to follow up with the referral. Oftentimes, you may have three or four dates listed as you get closer to setting up a firm meeting.

7. If you work in a profession which requires that, on occasion, you meet prospects at their homes or places of business, you should enter the directions to their homes or businesses on the back of the index card.

The index card contains all of the information concerning your referral. It provides you with easy access to this information and is laid out in a way that enables you to quickly access the data. Any small piece of information concerning your referral should be entered in section five. If you call a referral and his wife informs you that he is at baseball practice with his son, you should ask what would be a good time to reach him and enter that time and date in section six. You should then put a short note in section five reminding you that the prospect was at baseball practice with his son. On the surface this may seem unimportant. However, it may be the ice breaker that gets you in the door. You should be sure to mention that you had previously called while he was at the ballpark with his son. You may want to tell him that your son also plays baseball or that you coach baseball. You may want to ask him how old his boy is or if he has any other children who play ball. Any conversation you can spark that aids the process of making both your prospect and you feel more comfortable is of great use. Use section five wisely. It is one of the easiest ways to turn a warm referral into a hot one.

You may call a prospect on a Monday evening and be told by his spouse that he works late on Mondays and that the best time to reach him is on Wednesday evenings. When you follow up on Wednesday, you should tell him that you tried to call him on Monday night but that he was working and that his wife asked you to call back at this time. It is an open invitation to ask him what type of work he does. Without the information concerning his late night at work, it may be awkward to inquire about his profession. The recording of any and every piece of information regarding your prospect cannot be over-emphasized.

Use an index box to hold the cards. The box should contain two sets of dividers. The first set of dividers separates by months. The current month should be closest to the front with the other months following. The second set of dividers contains the numbers one through thirty-one. These should be filed directly behind the divider for the current month. As each day passes, the number for that day is removed and placed behind the divider for the next month following. This process continues until the last day of the month, when the final numbered card is placed behind the last day of the month in the next section and the old monthly divider is placed in the very end of all of the dividers.

As soon as you have entered on an index card the date you are required to follow up with a referral, you should place that index card behind the divider for the month you are to call him or her. If that month happens to be the current month, you would place it behind the date divider which contains the number that corresponds with your follow-up date. Every day, you should set a high priority on calling those prospects whose cards appear in the front of the box under the current date. At the beginning of a new month, you should separate your stack of cards for that month and put them behind the numbered day which corresponds to each index card.

In the very front of your box you should file the cards for prospects whom you have never contacted. If you have effectively utilized the information contained in this book, you will soon find that you need a second index card box to store cards for prospects whom you have not yet found time to contact. We call this a good problem to have.

Initially, you may find this difficult to imagine. I, myself, couldn't believe it when I had accumulated one and a half index card boxes of names I had never called. Very recently, I gave one of my associates fifty of these cards which I had originally collected two and a half years before. I had been in my business for one year and had no further need to prospect. My clients began doing it for me.

Whatever system you choose, make sure that you update it, on a daily basis, so that you do not fall behind. To leave information scattered on your desk on unrelated sheets of paper will become very confusing and you will lose valuable data.

The following is a short list of companies that specialize in the design of software which you may find of great use to help you manage your database of clients and prospects.

"Take Control Sales"
Brock Control Systems, Inc.   800-221-0775
2859 Paces Ferry Road, Suite 1000   404-431-1200
Atlanta, GA 30339

"Maximizer for Windows"
Modatech Systems International, Inc. 800-666-1510
8445 Freeport Parkway, Suite 535   214-929-7111
Irving, TX 75063

"Contact Plus"
Contact Plus Corporation   800-366-9876
Post Office Box 372577   407-779-4900
Satellite Beach, FL 32937

"Sales Ally"
Scherrer Resources, Inc.   800-950-0190
Wyndhill Professional Center   215-836-1830
8200 Plourtown Avenue
Philadelphia, PA 19118

"ClienTrak"
Vertex Software, Inc.   800-333-4845
3 Allegheny Center
Pittsburgh, PA 15212

"WinSales"
WinSales, Inc.   206-854-9580
25018 104th Avenue Southeast
Kent, WA 98031

"G2"
 Sirius Systems, Inc.   800-409-0826
Post Office Box 920639
Norcross, GA 30092

"E-Z Track"
E-Z Data, Inc.   800-777-9188
918 East Green Street
Pasadena, CA 91106

A Word from the Author

There are many thousands of professional golf-ers who have competed on the PGA tour. All of them have an uncanny ability to strike a golf ball with a tremendous degree of accuracy and consistency. Yet, of all these golfers, only a few have won a significant number of major tournaments. What these few have in common is a mindset geared toward winning. Getting referrals is also a state of mind requiring a mindset geared toward generating *future* business. During any encounter with a pros-pect or client, the parallel referral sale must become part of both your thought process and your sales presentation.

In any vocation, as in life, there is great value in education. The learning of new ideas, sales methods or product revisions is necessary for maintaining your credibility and professional growth. The profes-sion of selling is going through an accelerated phase of change. Selling skills that were very effective only a few years ago are rapidly becoming obsolete. How do you keep up with the latest developments in your profession? There is an outstanding source of information that I have found to be the best in the business: *Personal Selling Power*. This magazine contains three editorial sections that cover everything you need to stay on the cutting edge of sales success: knowledge, skills and motivation. The toll free number for *Personal Selling Power* is 800-752-7355. In Virginia, please call 703-752-7000.

This knowledge, while valuable, will do you absolutely no good unless you put it to use. Do not become one of those seminar, conference or convention attendees who are exposed to great ideas but don't use them. Put your knowledge into motion and you will be amazed at the results.

You, too, can double or triple your sales in a very short time. You, too, can work fewer hours while making more money. You, too, can lessen the amount of rejection to which you are subjected. If you study this book and make an honest effort to perfect the techniques contained herein, you, too, will soon begin EXPECTING REFERRALS!

Oh yes, before I forget, if you know anyone who you feel may appreciate my integrity and may benefit from reading this book ...

Scripts

F or your convenience, the scripts contained in this book have been assembed here. I feel that as a salesperson you should have your own unique way of phrasing and delivering your message. Read the following scripts out loud and make the appropriate adjustments as you feel necessary. It is important to personalize each script as this will help you become more comfortable and confident when speaking with both your prospects and clients.

Pre-Appointment Contact Phase
<u>Cold Referrals</u>

"Hello, is this Mr. Smith? ... My name is Scott Kramnick from Kramnick and Associates. How are you this evening? ... The reason I'm calling is because I'm working with families in 'The Pines,' helping them plan for the college education of their kids and I thought I'd give you a call to see if you would be

interested in chatting about the various options available to you. Is college planning something to which you've given much thought? ..."

OR

"Hello, is this Mrs. Smith? ... My name is Scott Kramnick from Kramnick Realty. How are you today? ... The reason I'm calling is because I am working with growing families in your area, who may be interested in the possibility of moving into a larger home. I thought I'd give you a call to find out if this is something you have considered and, if so, I would welcome the opportunity to represent you in finding the most qualified buyer for your home. Have you given much thought to looking for a larger home? ..."

OR

"Hello, is this Mr. Smith? ... My name is Scott Kramnick from Kramnick's Komputers. How are you this afternoon? ... The reason I'm calling is because I am helping many small businesses cut inventory and labor costs by making effective use of user friendly inventory management systems. I thought I'd give you a call to find out if you are already working with a systems consultant. And, if not, I would welcome the opportunity to stop by and give you some information that you may find of great value. Is this an area to which you've given much thought? ..."

Warm Referrals

"Hello, is this Ray? ... Hi, Ray, my name is Scott Kramnick from Kramnick and Associates. How are you this evening? ... John and Barbara Jones are clients of mine. I met with them a couple of weeks ago and shared some ideas concerning retirement planning and college planning. They were really excited about the services I had to offer and since I work strictly on referrals they were kind enough to mention that you might be interested in talking about college planning for your kids. What I would like to do is set up a time to chat with you and Dorothy about college planning or some of your other financial goals and show you some of the options available to help you achieve them. It's not really important to me that we do business; all I ask is if you appreciate the time we share together, if you feel that you benefit from the time we spend together, and, most important, if you respect my integrity, you would be willing to pass my name on to a friend or business associate who may also benefit from my services, just as John and Barbara did. Is that fair enough?"

OR

"Hello, is this Dorothy? ... Hi, Dorothy, my name is Scott Kramnick from Kramnick Realty. How are you today? ... John and Barbara Jones are clients of mine. I recently worked with them finding the most qualified buyer for their home and helped them choose a new home that satisfied all of their desires. They were really pleased with my service. And since I work strictly through referrals, they were kind

enough to mention that at some time you may benefit from the services I have to offer. I would like to set up a time to meet with you and Ray and leave you some information which I feel you will find of great value. It's not really important to me that we do business at this time. After all, the timing may not yet be appropriate for you to consider moving. It's not really important to me that we do business; all I ask is if you appreciate the time we share together, if you feel that you benefit from the time we spend together, and, most important, if you respect my integrity, you would be willing to pass my name on to a friend or business associate who may also benefit from my services, just as John and Barbara did. Is that fair enough?"

OR

"Hello, is this Ray? ... Hi, Ray, my name is Scott Kramnick from Kramnick's Komputers. How are you this afternoon? ... John and Barbara Jones are clients of mine. I met with them last week and helped them upgrade their database management system which they found to be a great savings for their business. They were really pleased with both my product and service. And since I work primarily through referrals, they were kind enough to mention that you might be interested in learning about the value I have to offer. I'd like to set up a time to stop by your store and share some ideas that you may find of great benefit. It's not really important to me that we do business; all I ask is if you appreciate the time we share together, if you feel that you benefit from the time we spend together, and, most important, if you respect my integrity, you

*would be willing to pass my name on to a friend or
business associate who may also benefit from my
services, just as John and Barbara did. Is that fair
enough?"*

Hot Referrals

*"Hello, is this Ray? ... Hi, Ray, this is Scott Kramnick
from Kramnick and Associates. How are you doing
this evening? ... The reason I'm calling is because
John and Barbara, besides being half-way decent
bridge players, are clients of mine. Since I work
strictly on referrals they were kind enough to mention
that you had expressed an interest in preparing for
your children's college education. What I would like
to do is set up a time to meet with you and Dorothy
and discuss the different options available. What
would be a good time for us to get together?"*

OR

*"Hello, is this Dorothy? ...Hi, Dorothy, this is Scott
Kramnick from Kramnick Realty. How are you doing
today? ... The reason I'm calling is because John and
Barbara, besides being half-way decent bridge players, are clients of mine. Since I work strictly on
referrals they were kind enough to mention that you
are considering moving into a larger home. What I
would like to do is set up a time to meet with you and
Ray to discuss the best way to find a qualified buyer
for your current home while we search for a new
home that fulfills your expectations. What would be
a good time for us to get together?"*

OR

"Hello, is this Ray? ... Hi, Ray, this is Scott Kramnick from Kramnick's Komputers. How are you doing today? ... The reason I'm calling is because John and Barbara, besides being half-way decent bridge players, are clients of mine. Since I work strictly on referrals they were kind enough to mention that you have considered upgrading your company's computer system. What I would like to do is set up a time to meet with you to discuss the various hardware and software products that you may find valuable in helping you achieve your business goals. What would be a good time for us to get together?"

Cutting Loose the Kind People

"Hello Joe, this is Scott Kramnick. How are you today?... Great. The reason I'm calling is because both you and I have been so busy lately that it has been impossible for us to set up a firm time to get together. Joe, most folks would probably continue to call you week after week until you get to the point where you become irritated. Because I work strictly through referrals, I don't want you to get upset with me. If Charlie ever found out that I was bugging you, I'm sure he'd never give me any more referrals. If you could do me a favor, I'd really appreciate it. I'm going to send you a brochure outlining my services, along with my business card. When your workload lightens up would you give me a call so that we can set up a time to meet? This way the next

time we talk, it will be at a time when it is convenient and comfortable for you. Is that fair enough?... Terrific. And please don't forget, if in the meanwhile you run into folks who you feel may benefit from my services, please give me a call and let me know who they are. Thanks a lot, I look forward to hearing from you soon."

Appointment Phase
Appointment Introduction

"What I'd like to do with you tonight is basically three things. First, I'd like to tell you a little bit about myself and my company so you will feel comfortable with whom you are doing business. Second, I'd like to hear about you so I feel comfortable in understanding exactly what your needs, desires and goals are. Then third, we will discuss the different options available to help you achieve your objectives. Is that fair enough?"

The Logic of Service

"If I take good care of you, then I hope you will be willing to pass my name on to other people who would appreciate the same honesty and integrity I have extended to you. I don't do this because I'm a good guy, or because I'm a good Christian; I do it because it makes good business sense. If I take care of you, you'll take care of me."

Building Relationships

"I am honored to have the opportunity to meet with you today. I am offering you more than a product or service. I am offering you a relationship which I am sure will continue to grow through the years."

OR

"My success and the success of my business is totally dependent upon getting quality referrals from my clients. I realize that you will introduce me to your friends, family and business associates only if the quality and integrity of the service I provide surpasses that to which you've grown accustomed. This I pledge."

Referral Gathering - Level One

"Oh! This is something very important. (Pass a legal pad and pen across the table to your clients.) *You know that I work strictly by referrals. Would you be kind enough to write down the names of a few folks who might benefit from my services? You don't need to worry about how much money they make or if you think they may already have satisfied their goals. What I'll do is give them a call and treat them the same way I treated you. I'll explain to them that it is not important to me that we do business. All that matters is that if they appreciate the time we share together, if they respect my integrity, and if they feel that they learned something during our meeting, that they will be willing to pass my name on to someone else who may benefit from my services. I really*

appreciate this. I depend on good clients, like you, to keep my business rolling."

Referral Gathering - Level Two

"You know that I work strictly by referrals. (You pass them a legal pad. As they begin to write the names of people they know you continue speaking.) *Would you be kind enough to write down the names of a few folks who might benefit from my services? You don't need to worry about how much money they make or if you think they may already have satisfied their goals. It would mean a lot to me if over the next week you would mention to these folks that you were very pleased with my services and that it may be in their best interest to set up a time to meet with me. In about a week I'll give you a call and you can let me know which of these folks seem the most interested. I promise you that I will treat each of your referrals with the same respect and integrity that I have extended to you. I'll explain to them that it is not important to me that we do business. I'll tell them all that matters is if they appreciate the time we share together, if they respect my integrity, and if they feel they learned something during our meeting, they will be willing to pass my name on to someone else who may benefit from my services. I really appreciate this. I depend on good clients, like you, to keep my business rolling."*

Referral Gathering - Level Three

"You know that I work strictly by referrals. **I would be honored if you would do me a favor and give some**

of your friends, family and business associates one of my brochures. (You pass them several brochures.) *It would be really helpful to me if you would take a moment to explain to them how much you value my service and that you feel they may benefit from meeting with me. Please make a mental note of anyone who seemed interested. I will not burden you by asking you for a list of names, but if you would be kind enough to allow me to give you a call next week and get the names of those interested individuals, I would greatly appreciate it.* I promise you I will treat any referrals you give me with the same respect and dignity that I have treated you. I'll explain to them that it is not important to me that we do business. I'll tell them all that matters is if they appreciate the time we share together, if they respect my integrity, and if they feel they learned something during our meeting, they will be willing to pass my name on to someone else who may benefit from my services. I really appreciate this. I depend on good clients, like you, to keep my business rolling."

Referral Gathering - Level Four

"You know that I work strictly by referrals. I would be honored if you would do me a favor and give some of your friends, family and business associates one of my brochures. (You pass them several brochures.) *It would be really helpful to me if you would take a moment to explain to them how much you value my service and that you feel they may benefit from meeting with me. Please make a mental note of anyone who seemed interested. I will not burden you by asking you for a list of names, but if you would be kind enough to call me with the names of anyone who seemed interested I would greatly appreciate it. I promise you I will treat any referrals you give me with the same respect and dignity that I have treated you. I'll explain to them that it is not important to me that we do business. I'll tell them all that matters is if they appreciate the time we share together, if they respect my integrity, and if they feel they learned something during our meeting, they will be willing to pass my name on to someone else who may benefit from my services. I really appreciate this. I depend on good clients, like you, to keep my business rolling."*

Referral Gathering - Level Five

"You know that I work strictly by referrals. I would be honored if you would do me a favor and give some of your friends, family and business associates one of my brochures. (You pass them several brochures.) It would be really helpful to me if you would take a moment to explain to them how much you value my service and that you feel they may benefit from meeting with me. I will not burden you by asking for a list of names. But I would ask, once again, that you encourage your friends, family members, and business associates to call me. I promise you I will treat any referrals you give me with the same respect and dignity that I have treated you. I'll explain to them that it is not important to me that we do business. I'll tell them all that matters is if they appreciate the time we share together, if they respect my integrity, and if they feel they learned something during our meeting, they will be willing to pass my name on to someone else who may benefit from my services. I really

appreciate this. I depend on good clients, like you, to keep my business rolling."

Product Delivery
Strengthening Relationships

"I want you to know that I value your trust in me and I look forward to providing you with the best service possible. If you ever have any questions or need any advice on how to make the best use of your purchase, please call me. Here is my home telephone number. If it happens to be after hours, please don't hesitate to call me there. It is important to me that you know I stand behind my product one hundred percent and I will do anything in my power to keep you as a satisfied client."

The Improvement Question

"I'm sure by now you realize that I work strictly through referrals. I am constantly striving to bring my clients even greater service by improving my business. I have a very important question for you and would appreciate your giving this some thought. Is there any one thing that you would like to see me change or improve upon which would increase the likelihood of my getting referrals from you in the future?"

Referral Status Report

"I appreciate the opportunity of doing business with you. I know that you are very happy with the service I have provided you and I promise to be here should

you have any questions or need further help in the future. I'd like to thank you for sharing your friends, Ray and Dorothy, with me. I met with them last week and I'm sure they told you that they were very happy with the time we shared together. It really means a lot to me that you trust me enough to share the names of some of your friends and business associates with me. As I promised you in the past, I will never say anything or treat the referrals you give me in a way that would cause a bad reflection on you. Obviously, you would never provide me with another referral. I look forward to a longlasting relationship with both you and with anyone else I meet. Which reminds me, I haven't had a chance to meet the Johnsons yet. Could you tell me when might be the best time to contact them?"

"Have you had a chance to hand out any of my brochures to your friends or have you talked with anyone about the services I have to offer? ... What was their reaction?"

Service and Follow-Up
Annual Follow-Up

"Hello, Ray. This is Scott Kramnick. How are you? ... As I promised, when we first did business, this is my 'official' once-a-year call to let you know that I haven't forgotten about you. You should have received your annual report by now. Do you have any questions? ...I also want to make sure you and Dorothy have received your birthday cards and quarterly newsletters. What do you think of my newsletter? ...Terrific. I'll let you go now, don't forget,

you've got my number if you need any help. Please keep me in mind when talking to your friends and business associates. As you know, Ray, I depend on quality clients like you and Dorothy to keep me in business. I look forward to seeing you soon. Goodbye."

Just A Note

Dear Joe,
Just a quick note to let you know it's been an honor over the past year to have the opportunity to play a small part in helping you achieve your goals. Thanks for referring Ray and Dorothy to me. I promise to provide them with the same quality service I have extended to you. I look forward to seeing you soon.
Best Wishes,
Scott

Referral Enhancement
Learning from Mistakes

"Ray, as you know, I work strictly through referrals and depend upon quality clients like yourself to help me grow my business. I sense that you feel uncomfortable providing me with names of people you know. I'm convinced that you believe in my product and service. Have I done something to lose your trust?"

The Deli Method

Salesperson: *"Ray, I know you appreciate the time that I have spent with you this afternoon. Would you mind giving me the name of someone who might also* *appreciate the same integrity that I have extended to you? Just a first name would be fine."*

Ray: *"Well, you might want to talk to Tim."*

Salesperson: *"And who else?"*

Ray: *"Well, I work with a guy named Jack."*

Salesperson: *"And who else?"*

Ray: *"My brother, Steve."*

Salesperson: *"And who else?"*

Capitalizing on Good Feelings

"Hi Ray... I'm glad to hear you're happy with the business we've done together. Ray, by now you certainly know that I work strictly by referrals. Would you happen to know anyone else you feel may benefit from the value I've extended to you? It would mean a lot to me if you could share the names of a couple of folks whom I promise to treat with the utmost respect. How about one of the companies you do business with? Is there anyone who you feel can benefit from the services I offer?"

Information Enhancement

"Ray, I thank you for giving me Joe's name. Would you mind telling me if he is married or has any children? ...Is it best to contact Joe at home or do you think he may prefer I call him at work? ...What type

of work does he do? ...How did you folks meet? ...Which of the services I offer do you feel he would find of greatest value?"

Alleviating Qualifications

"Ray, would you happen to know anyone who may benefit from my services? It's important that you don't try to qualify them by how much money they make. You know that I work strictly through referrals and I must tell you that some of my largest client accounts have come from the parents, friends or bosses of my clients with small accounts. Whom might you know who could benefit from my service?"

Appendix B

Objections to Giving Referrals

Whena product or service is being solicited, salespeople pay very close attention to any objections their clients may have. Salespeople have been trained to both present their product in such a way that few objections will surface and to effectively respond to any objections that may arise. For the most part, very few salespeople have been properly educated in the ways to overcome a client's objections to giving referrals.

Just as the sales presentation is geared toward overcoming product objections before they materialize, the parallel referral sale must also identify any referral objections before they arise. A good salesperson is a master of sensing any possible objections and soothing the client's concerns before they become a matter of debate. The following paragraphs identify some of the most common objections clients may have with giving referrals and provide ideas that you will find useful in helping you to overcome them.

Clients are afraid of upsetting friends and relatives.

This is the most common concern clients have when considering providing a salesperson with referrals. Clients fear that the passing on of names may not be appreciated by their friends, family or business associates. These fears are often deep-rooted and with merit. Because of over-aggressive behavior and lack of sensitivity, many salespeople have contributed to a stereotype which is considerably less than favorable. It is important that you create a distinction, in the minds of your clients, between you and the typical salesperson. In the Appointment phase of the Referral Cycle, the time during which you have the most personal contact with your clients, you must let them know that you will be treating their referrals with the same respect and courtesy that you have extended to them. When asking for referrals I tell my clients, up front and honestly, that they do not have to worry about my upsetting any referrals they give me. I tell my clients that if their referrals are not interested in chatting with me when I make the initial contact, I will immediately back down and thank them for their time. I also remind my clients about the pleasant experience they had during our initial contact. I pledge to treat their referrals with the same dignity.

Clients feel finances are personal in nature.

Whether your clients have purchased a product, made an investment, or contracted your services, it is important that they know that the specific nature of their purchase will not be revealed to the referrals they provided you. Clients must know that the business they have undertaken with you will be handled with the utmost confidentiality. I always tell my clients that I will not reveal anything concerning their family or finances to their referrals. I never take for granted that this confidentiality is already assumed by my clients. Once again, I bring this point up during the Appointment phase of the Referral Cycle and well before it ever surfaces as an objection. It is important that you respect people's privacy.

Clients do not want friends to think they are being discussed.

People do not like the thought of someone talking about them behind their back. Oftentimes, clients will not want to give you names because they fear that their referrals may get the impression that their personal matters were being discussed during the appointment. This is a very fine point and is, once again, easily handled during the Appointment phase of the Referral Cycle. I tell my clients that when I contact the referrals they have given me, I will say that I work strictly by referrals and that their friends were kind enough to mention that they may be interested in chatting with me. I also tell my clients that I will treat their referrals in the same manner in which I treated them.

Clients tend to qualify their friends by income or class.

Clients will frequently pre-qualify their friends, family or business associates before considering them to be eligible for your services. It is important that your clients know that you have the capability of providing service to people who are both above and below their perceived financial status. For example, when a client gives me $10,000 to invest in a mutual fund, I always take the time to explain that it is also possible to invest as little as $25 a month. My clients may know a few people who they think may be able to afford $10,000, but they probably know many more people who would be able to afford $25 a month. Too many salespeople ignore the "little guys." I don't. It is important that you tell your clients not to pre-qualify anyone. Make sure they understand that you have a wide variety of services to offer that can accommodate everyone, even their friends who are *"loaded"*!

Clients, in general, look down upon salespeople.

Your job here is to separate yourself from the stereotypical salesperson. If you treat your clients with sincerity, respect and dignity, they will look up to you and open doors that you never dreamed possible. Don't forget the information contained in the chapter "Understanding Attitudes." Your clients often have a stereotypical view of salespeople. You must create a difference between yourself and your competition. It is critical that you point out this difference to your clients.

Clients may believe in the product but not in the salesperson.

Sometimes clients will purchase a product or service that they feel is of value, but will not provide referrals. They buy because of the product - not because of the salesperson. Your clients must believe in you before they give you referrals. It is important that you sell yourself and the benefits you have to offer while you are selling your product or service and the benefits it has to offer.

Clients fear the salesperson may not be around years down the road.

Tell your clients that you will be around years down the road ... *especially* when they give you referrals. I always tell my clients that referrals are my sole method of prospecting and that I have been blessed with good clients who keep me in business by passing my name along to their friends, family and business associates. It is important to drive a good car and have a nice office in a professional location. Very few people feel comfortable giving referrals to somebody who lacks an aura of success.

Clients do not feel they can benefit from giving the salesperson referrals.

I tell my clients that they will benefit in two ways by giving me referrals. First, as discussed above, I will remain in business and be able to provide them with continued service. Second, they will be held in high esteem by their friends, family or business associates who have had the opportunity to do business with me. This may seem a little bit egotistical. It is. But if I don't believe in myself, they won't believe in me.

Clients may not know anyone to refer.

This is simply not true. If clients tell you they do not know anyone they are really saying one of two things. First, it may be that they cannot *think* of anyone. If this occurs then it is necessary for you to help jar your clients' memories. Asking them if they have any brothers or sisters, if they have anyone they work closely with, or if they know any of their neighbors are but a few of the ideas you may use. You may also ask them if they attend church or are members of any local organizations. Both of these latter examples tend to be excellent sources of referrals.

Second, they may be tactfully trying to tell you that they don't want to give you any referrals. They are being kind enough to say it in a way that they hope will not hurt your feelings. If you have followed the procedures outlined in this book and have remained sensitive to your clients' emotions, this will not happen to you.

The key to overcoming each of these objections is to be aware of their existence from the first moment you have contact with your clients. It is important that you memorize each of these concerns and make a concerted effort to address each of them individually throughout the Referral Cycle. Once again, I will mention that overcoming objections is always a key to selling a product or service. It is also the key to getting referrals.

Public Law 102-243

One Hundred Second Congress of the United States of America

AT THE FIRST SESSION

Begun and held at the City of Washington on Thursday the third day of January, one thousand nine hundred and ninety-one

AN ACT

To amend the Communications Act of 1934 to prohibit certain practices involving the use of telephone equipment.

Be it enacted by the Senate and House of Representatives of the United States of America in Congress assembled.

SECTION 1. SHORT TITLE.

This Act may be cited as the "Telephone Consumer Protection Act of 1991."

SECTION 2. FINDINGS.

The Congress finds that:

(1) The use of the telephone to market goods and services to the home and other businesses is now pervasive due to the increased use of cost-effective telemarketing techniques.

(2) Over 30,000 businesses actively telemarket goods and services to business and residential customers.

(3) More than 300,000 solicitors call more than 18,000,000 Americans every day.

(4) Total United States sales generated through telemarketing amounted to $435,000,000,000 in 1990, a more than four-fold increase since 1984.

(5) Unrestricted telemarketing, however, can be an intrusive invasion of privacy and, when an emergency or medical assistance telephone line is seized, a risk to public safety.

(6) Many consumers are outraged over the proliferation of intrusive, nuisance calls to their homes from telemarketers.

(7) Over half the States now have statutes restricting various uses of the telephone for marketing, but telemarketers can evade their prohibitions through interstate operations; therefore, Federal law is needed to control residential telemarketing practices.

(8) The Constitution does not prohibit restrictions on commercial telemarketing solicitations.

(9) Individuals' privacy rights, public safety interest, and commercial freedoms of speech and trade must be balanced in a way that protects the privacy of individuals and permits legitimate telemarketing practices.

(10) Evidence compiled by the Congress indicates that residential telephone subscribers consider automated or prerecorded telephone calls, regardless of the content or the initiator of the message, to be a nuisance and an invasion of privacy.

(11) Technologies that might allow consumers to avoid receiving such calls are not universally available, are costly, are unlikely to be enforced, or place an inordinate burden on the consumer.

(12) Banning such automated or prerecorded telephone calls to the home, except when the receiving party consents to receiving the call or when such calls are necessary in an emergency situation affecting the health and safety of the consumer, is the only effective means of protecting telephone consumers from this nuisance and privacy invasion.

(13) While the evidence presented to the Congress indicates that automated or prerecorded calls are a nuisance and an invasion of privacy, regardless of the type of call, the Federal Communications Commission should have the flexibility to design different rules for those types of automated or

prerecorded calls that it finds are not considered a nuisance or invasion of privacy, or for noncommercial calls, consistent with the free speech protections embodied in the First Amendment of the Constitution.

(14) Businesses also have complained to the Congress and the Federal Communications Commission that automated or prerecorded telephone calls are a nuisance, are an invasion of privacy, and interfere with interstate commerce.

(15) The Federal Communications Commission should consider adopting reasonable restrictions on automated or prerecorded calls to businesses as well as to the home, consistent with the Constitutional protections of free speech.

Index

If you would like information on multiple book discounts or if you may be interested in scheduling Scott Kramnick for a speech, seminar or workshop, please call or write to:

Kramnick & Associates, Inc.
4300 Plank Road, Suite 280
Fredericksburg, VA 22407
(800)786-9799
or
(703)786-9799